Interreligious Life Issues

Interfaith Treasures Uncovered

Under this Series, the Publishers endeavor to focus on Comparative Studies pertaining to Christian Faith & Living in the central matrix and Hinduism, Buddhism, Sikhism, Islam, Judaism, etc., on the peripheral. The Studies shall cover topics like Literature & Poetry, Indigenous Philosophizing, Ethical response towards Agriculture, Health & Healing, Science & Technology, Ecofeminist Theology, Sociological approach towards Human Rights, Law & Politics, Arts, History of Ideas, Ancient Civilizations, Cultural Contiguity, Religious Cosmologies & Mysticism, Footsteps of famous Theologians, World Peace & Harmony, Global Capitalism, Network Marketing, Cybertheology, Population & Demographics, Epigraphic Studies, Contextualized Education, and many others. We welcome a Mss. on any topic/s mentioned, whether they are original works, scholarly monographs, collections of conference papers, revised dissertations, or translations of historical documents. Through the Series, we are striving to put forward published works that may help Institutions, Academic Bodies, Researchers, Scholars and the World at large in furthering their respective knowledge and understanding on the concerned subject. We welcome your comments on our efforts and further suggestions on how we can foster the upcoming books on parallel interfaces between and among Christianity and other religions.

Interfaith Treasures Uncovered - 17

Interreligious Life Issues

Relationship, Education, Prayer,
Marriage, Funeral and Engagement

Israel Selvanayagam

CWI

Christian World Imprints

First Published in 2019 by

Christian World Imprints
Christian Publishing & Books from India
H-12 Bali Nagar, **New Delhi-110015**
info@christianworldimprints.com
www.ChristianWorldImprints.com
Phone: +91 11 25465925

ISBN: 978-93-5148-313-7

Cataloging in Publication Data--DK
Courtesy: D.K. Agencies (P) Ltd. <docinfo@dkagencies.com>

Celvanāyakam, Israyēl, author.
Interreligious life issues : relationship, education, prayer, marriage, funeral and engagement / Israel Selvanayagam.
pages cm. -- (Interfaith treasures uncovered ; 17)
ISBN 9789351483137

1. Religions--Relations. 2. Interfaith marriage--India. 3. Interfaith worship--India. 4. India--Religion. I. Title. II. Series: Interfaith treasures uncovered ; 17.

LCC BL410.C45 2019 | DDC 201.5 23

Printed in India.

Prof. S. Jeyapragasam (1949-2018) was a Gandhian and former head of the Department of the Philosophy of Gandhi and Ramalinga Swamy of the Madurai Kamaraj University. He organised the weekly interreligious prayer at Gandhi Museum, Madurai, promoted interreligious understanding and advocated peace and non-violence through meetings and literature. He collaborated with other programmes of dialogue including that of the Tamilnadu Theological Seminary. His kindness, humility and integrity made him a fascinating friend and guru. I am pleased to dedicate this book to his memory.

Foreword

I first went to India in 1975, with my wife Angela, and two young daughters, to Madurai, in the heart of Tamil Nadu, 300 miles south of Madras, now Chennai. I went to join the teaching faculty of the Tamil Nadu Theological Seminary. An Indian colleague invited me to come, and said, come and teach something, but you will learn much more from being with us. This was the case, as my life, and that of my family, was transformed by my seven years at the seminary, within this major Hindu city. I learnt much from the context. This has been with me ever since. But, I learnt above all from fellow staff, and from students training there to be pastors in a multi faith context. Israel Selvanayagam was outstanding in both areas. I returned to U.K. and spent the rest of my ministry in theological teaching, but also in learning from the transformed context in Britain, increasingly multi-religious and multi-cultural, and helping my students to engage with this reality, and indeed to be excited by the possibilities in front of them.

Israel was a final year student when we arrived, and I have been alongside him in the ensuing four decades. He is one of those from whom I have learnt the most. He followed me to England, when I was asked to recommend a South Indian to teach in the Methodist ministerial training institution (Wesley College) in Bristol. From there he had links with Queen's College, in Birmingham, where I was on the staff. And then he followed me as Principal of the United College of the Ascension, a mission training college, in Selly Oak, also in Birmingham. After two years of two part timeworks (minister of two churches in East Birmingham and interfaith consultant for the District) he returned to India in 2008 as his heart was for his own country and church. Having been again in theological education in Bangalore and Chennai Israel returned to the Methodist Church in Britain, to be a circuit minister in Evesham, a very English context, from where he has put together this book.

Interreligious Life Issues is a very rich book, suitable for those who are much experienced in interfaith work, and those who are at the beginning of their learning journey. It covers some vital themes of engagement, and Israel manages to combine in a balanced way, the experiences that come out of South India, that are the bedrock of his ministry, with the British context, where he has now also spent many years. He has also taken part in major international gatherings on interfaith themes, including those of the WCC. He brings together a range of beautiful examples, and stories, within each chapter, as he roots big themes in the practice of ministry and mission. And his writing is never abstract. He has lived these great themes. In addition, he shows his breadth of learning and reading, with the range of writings referred to, from India, and from the west.

The book is comprehensive in the way Israel draws upon his knowledge of all the main religions of India, as he applies this to the broad themes. These are largely pastoral themes- marriage, prayer, death, engagement, education, relationships. Israel is very conversant with the main theological themes of interfaith dialogue, but for him, this is never abstract theory, but applied theology, in terms of mission and ministry. He is rightly suspicious, if interreligious dialogue is practiced simply as a means to prepare for the hard end of evangelism and conversion. But he is a minister deeply rooted in Christ, and in the Christian scriptures, on the basis of which he engages with the great themes in the book.

I have no hesitation in commending this book. I was much influenced myself by Israel, when I wrote my first book- *Encounter in the Spirit: Muslim-Christian Dialogue in Birmingham.'* There are many *encounters in the Spirit* recorded in this book. I also see Israel primarily as a teacher, as well as a preacher of the gospel, and this is what he can be seen practicing throughout this book. I hope it will be accessible to many here, and help them to combine theology and scripture, with engagement in mission across religious communities. It will be a great resource for them. Hopefully it can be used too in theological training, both in the UK and in India.

Canon Dr. Andrew Wingate, OBE
Hon. Inter Faith Adviser to the Diocese of Chichester
East Sussex

Preface

It was in February 1977 that I was persuaded by my mentors, particularly Dr. Samuel Amirtham, to take up the new 'ministry' of interreligious dialogue. This was while preparing to go back to my diocese (Kanyakumari) after completing four years of my theological education and ministerial training at Tamilnadu Theological Seminary, Madurai. The initial feeling was bitter to switch over from the respected pastoral ministry to somewhat suspect dialogue ministry. It was an uncharted journey outside the camp without clear expectations and goals. Now it is history. Starting with visiting devotees in their worship places and organising the monthly Religious Friends Circle, my ministry expanded to different directions. For all the subsequent years in my both pastoral and teaching ministry, with additional responsibilities in Jail Ministry, Theological Education for Christian Commitment and Action and in editing theological text-books based in TTS, an interreligious focus has been consistent. I have not found any compelling reason to give up the Christian ministry for which I had been called in 1969.

The combination of Christian ministry, both pastoral and teaching and ministry of dialogue, has been most exciting although there have been moments of frustration and even despondency. There seemed to be a deficit of openness to understanding and civility. There were many opportunities to be part of national and international consultations. Calculation of loss and gain is not applicable here, but one thing is certain, that it has helped to have more in-depth knowledge of the scriptures and experiences of people of other religions. More significantly, experience of interreligious dialogue has helped me to understand the perceptions outsiders have about Christianity. I have shown here and there how badly we are influenced by the notions and practices of other religions, particularly the Hindu religious traditions, and failed to convey the unique message of the gospel. This set my heart on fire to work to reform the church and make it truly evangelical. However, although there has been no resistance, there has been the act of ignoring. Martin Luther's reformation is uncritically glorified without incorporating its creative side for reforming the Indian church.

Perceptions of interreligious relationships differ from person to person. Those who designed courses on study of religions in the theological curricula of the Senate of Serampore College (University, from 1910), at least in the early decades, expected that this study would equip the ministerial candidates for sensible mission. Many wanted to use the knowledge to score points for the Christian message and to dialogue/argue with people of other religions with a hidden agenda to win them over. Then some pastoral scholars insisted on understanding people of other religions as they understand themselves and on forging genuine relationships for dialogue. But there have been thorny difficulties. Not all the persons of other religions have a fair amount of basic knowledge of their own beliefs and practices. To some extent, this is true of Christians as well. Conservative and fundamentalist Christians have openly declared that dialogue is a satanic movement, an aberration of Christian commitment and a trap to stumble, confuse and mislead innocent, pure and simpleminded Christians. Theories developed by scholars based in western universities have very limited relevance for the Indian situation. At the same in India, scholarly study of religions is mainly done by Christian institutions and it is not reciprocated and paralleled by others. Departments of Philosophy in Indian universities do not show interest in real comparative study of religion and its application to socio-economic realities. Occasional interreligious conversations and worship cannot be a substitute for tackling the multi-headed monsters such as poverty, corruption and untouchability in the otherwise great country of India.

When I moved to the United Kingdom on the invitation of the Methodist Church in 1996, I encountered new realities on the interreligious front. Based in Bristol, I taught mainly at the Wesley College and partly Queen's College, Birmingham, a more multi-religious city. There were a number of interreligious programmes going on, but most if not all of which were organised by Christian churches and institutions. My friend and colleague, Andrew Wingate who had been challenged and equipped by the programmes of interreligious dialogue in TTS (1975-1982), on his return to Birmingham did some pioneering work in forging interreligious relations and facilitating dialogue. In Bristol, I took student groups to places of worship, particularly the Methodist church-converted Hindu temple (*Sanatan Mandhir*), and we regularly attended the civic celebrations organised by the local council where we could meet representatives of other religious communities. It was conspicuous that people of other religions, mostly recent migrants, experienced lack of welcome, indifference, rejection, disrespect and even hostility. Though those who reacted in this way were not churchgoing Christians, some churches had the courage to expose this terrible attitude, confessing racism and growing homophobia among the English people. Then, Hindus, Muslims, Buddhists, Sikhs, Zoroastrians and Baha'is went into defence mode and became apologetic in meetings; opportunity for genuine dialogue was lost. My initiative to bring together an interreligious group for sustained dialogue in Wesley College failed. However, student groups who went on placement in India came back excited with questions about overwhelming religiosity and problems of poverty, untouchability and ultra-conservative trends within the Church in India.

I started my new job as the Principal of the United College of the Ascension in January 2001 (succeeding Andrew Wingate). Ecumenical, international and inter-cultural, a world church community was living and worshipping together, following different study and training programmes. Any interreligious gathering was both exciting and controversial. Though it was seriously a mission college with the slogan 'from everywhere to everywhere', some inmates thought that the college was going away from the Christ centre and they had no hesitation in saying this openly in prayers. At the same time, some innovative events I organised proved to be an eye-opener. For example, once a group representing other religious communities in Birmingham were asked to comment on Jesus' claim 'I am the way and the truth and the life. No one comes to the Father except through me' (Jn. 14: 6). The comments included the following: this verse was a later addition; Jesus as a matured and saintly person would not have said this; the words 'way, truth and life' do not suggest an easy approach to salvation.

From 2006-2008 I was part-time Interfaith Consultant in the Birmingham District of the Methodist Church and part-time minister of two Methodist congregations in multi-cultural East Birmingham. The highlight of the first role was to conduct a series of study programmes called 'Re-reading the Bible in Multi-Religious Context.' The response and result were most encouraging. There was not much scope to build up relationships with people of other religions. However, a group witnessing to a mid-week Eucharist and the discussion afterwards was memorable.

I returned to India in 2008 and after a brief period at United Theological College and a break, I taught at the Gurukul Lutheran Theological College and Research Institute, Chennai. Encouraged by colleagues there, under the inter-disciplinary course a seminar on issues in interreligious relations was offered for the second year MTh students. There were also a few doctoral dissertations which touched upon dialogue. There had been initiatives for establishing a programme on interfaith dialogue in the college. Guidelines were drawn and approved by the faculty. However, apart from a few events, the programme could not be sustained. At the same time, there were consultations and conferences organized by Catholic institutions such as the Department of Christian Studies of the University of Madras and Institute of Dialogue with Cultures and Religions (Loyola College). As a group of faculty and students, we were the most favoured guests who could contribute and learn. The idea for working towards a Chennai Interfaith Forum was being floated. My term came to an end in March 2016. Currently I am based in the Methodist Church in Evesham. Although, there are not many persons of other religions in this English town, I am associated with the nearby Worcester Interfaith Forum and attend select events in Birmingham.

A Christian seriously engaged in interreligious dialogue with a special commitment to understanding and communication is expected to write and publish. My higher studies have been in the area of Religion and Religions, mainly the Hindu religious traditions, and I have published in this area considerably. As far as the area of interreligious dialogue is concerned, mention of the main publications may give a helpful understanding for following this book: *A Dialogue on Dialogue: Preliminary Reflections on Interfaith Encounters* (1995) and its follow up *A Second Call: Ministry and Mission in a Multi-faith Milieu* (2000). I was encouraged by Dr. Dayanandan Francis (1932-2007) who in the initial years guided me in the ministry of dialogue. We decided to dedicate *A Second Call* to Bishop Selvamony (1915-2010) who pioneered dialogue in TTS, and who when he became the bishop in Kanyakumari diocese (1973) made history by appointing a full-time minister of dialogue. *A Second Call* has been out of print for several years. Copies in libraries have the marks of overuse, and parts of it have been photocopied. I revised the text for a second edition but the original publisher (CLS) expressed inability, yet encouraging me to publish elsewhere. Since its original publication, I have published elaborate versions of two of its chapters: *Relating to People of Other Faiths: Insights from the Bible* (2004) and *Being Evangelical and Dialogical: A Healthy Balance in a Multi-faith Context* (2012). For academic and pastoral purposes, the most in demand have been materials on interreligious education, prayer, marriage, and funerals. I have revised them and added two more chapters, first and last, hence this book.

I am consciously using the word 'interreligious', a departure from the popular usage of 'interfaith'. This is for the sake of clarity. It was regarded in the 1970s a major shift to use 'interfaith' following ecumenical titles such as *Faith in the Midst of Faiths* and *Faith Meets Faith.* I think 'religion' is commonly and comfortably general and inclusive and 'faith' specific, although interchange is not impossible depending on the understanding and usage of the terms. Religion (= that which binds together) is multi-dimensional: mythical, ritual, experiential and so on, and evident in all religions with varying meanings and magnitude. From that comes the word 'religiosity' which transcends particular religion. Religiosity is extended to mean sacred sense, transcendent awareness and so on. In this sense all humans in one way or other are religious even if they profess a secular ideology like humanism. As far as the theistic religions are concerned, faith is normally understood as trust in God, reliance on God and confidence in the future guided by God. But there is a special understanding of faith in the Christian scriptures. Jesus pointed out it as the ability to move 'mountains', daring to remove challenging blockades, trying the impossible and achieving something by transgressing normal conditions and customary practices. The act of a few in this sense is identified as *faith* in certain people of other religions too. Paul brings out a new meaning, i.e., accepting that God has accepted us in Christ though we are unacceptable. The writer to the Hebrews presents 'clouds of witnesses' who by faith achieved great things in solidarity with the suffering of others while foregoing their own pleasure.

The Arabic word *din* 'covers a semantic range which includes religion, judgment and conduct.' Muslims use the more popular word *iman* in the main sense of a deep conviction about the ultimate truth of Allah's commands and submission to his will. Buddhists use faith in terms of their trust in Buddha's experience of enlightenment and teaching. In brahmanic Hinduism, connected to truth, trust or faith (*sraddha*) means, the ritual faith 'in terms of the full confidence of the sacrificer in the efficacy of the rite, competence of the priests, power of the mantras and in the ability of the gods.' Non-brahmanic traditions with regional variety may use near synonyms in the vernacular. Those who have basic knowledge about these religions and engage in serious dialogue with their adherents may well come to the conclusion to make a distinction between religion and faith. The concern is that we need to have basic clarity about the terms we use and that we should not impose one religion's specific words (for example, the Christian understanding of faith) on the other. If this discussion is unnecessarily complicating, particular groups of dialogue may decide on a particular term. Vision and mysticism may offer yet other alternatives. It is no one's fault if the whole thing looks complicated because, after all, religion itself is complex and varied.

I have tried to be as authentic and limited in scope as possible. The six issues dealt with here can be elaborated taking the views and practices of religions, traditions and sects with their regional variety. I have lived between the cultures of India and the United Kingdom, and therefore the examples are predominantly from these two countries. It is my hope that these examples and reflections will help prospective students and practitioners of interreligious dialogue.

It is my duty to acknowledge those who have enriched this book. Since 1977 Andrew Wingate has been a valuable friend and colleague in the ministry of interreligious relations and dialogue. Inspired by what he saw in TTS, he initiated number of programmes in Birmingham and the climax was the establishment in the multi-religious city Leicester of St Philips Centre which is about 'learning to live well together' with the components of encounter, co-operation, trust and understanding. Therefore, I thought that he should be the most suitable person to write a foreword to this book. I am immensely grateful to him.

As before, William Allberry, a prominent member of the Friends of Church in India (based in UK), has checked the language, refined the word processing, offered comments and raised questions for clarity. I am grateful for his patience and engaging reading.

I remember with gratitude Benjamin Inbaraj, former General Secretary of the Christian Literature Society, Chennai, for encouraging to publish the revised version of the *A Second Call: Ministry and Mission in a Multi-faith Milieu.* When I approached the Christian World Imprints, as usual, Mr. Sudhanshu Kanda promptly sent a positive reply and has overseen the process with meticulous care. I thank him and his staff.

While completing the draft of this book I received the sad news that Prof. S. Jeyapragasam (1949-2018) of Madurai passed away. He was a Gandhian and former head of the Department of the Philosophy of Gandhi and Ramalinga Swamy of the Madurai Kamaraj University. He organized the weekly interreligious prayer at Gandhi Museum and a good supporter of the programme on Interfaith Dialogue of TTS which, he claimed, inspired him to initiate dialogues. His kindness, humility and integrity made him a fascinating friend. I am pleased to dedicate this book to his memory.

By definition relationship and dialogue cannot be static and doctrinal. I hope that all those serious readers of this book will gain new insights for their ongoing journey of life and pursuit of truth.

India's Independence Day, 15 August 2018
Evesham, England

Abbreviations

BCC	British Council of Churches
BD	Batchelor of Divinity
BRE	Batchelor of Religious Education
BTh	Batchelor of Theology
BTESSC	Board of Theological Education of the Senate of Serampore College
BTTBPSA	Board of Theological Text-Book Programme of South Asia
CCBI	Council of Churches in Britain and Ireland
CCJ	Council of Christians and Jews
CCJP	Committee on the Church and Jewish People
CISRS	Christian Institute for the Study of Religion and Society (Bangalore and New Delhi)
CLS	Christian Literature Society (Madras)
CPWR	Council for a Parliament of the World's Religions
CSI	Church of South India
CWME	Commission on World Mission and Evangelism (WCC)

DMK	'Dravidian Progressive Movement' (*Thiraavida Munnaetra Kazhakam*)
DTh	Doctor of Theology
IMC	International Missionary Council
MEET	Multi-faith Education by Extension in Tamilnadu
MTh	Master of Theology
OIRR	Office on Inter-Religious Relations (WCC)
PCID	Pontifical Council for Interfaith Dialogue (Vatican)
RFC	Religious Friends Circle (TTS)
SICMan	South India Churchman
TTS	Tamilnadu Theological Seminary (Madurai)
UTC	United Theological College (Bangalore)
WCC	World Council of Churches (Geneva)
WMC	World Missionary Conference

Chapter 1

Interreligious Relationship

The Meaning of Relationship

Is it not unnecessary to define the meaning of 'relationship', since it is most obvious and understandable? The root of the word suggests a state of being related, connected or associated. There are emotional and contractual aspects in a serious relationship such as marriage; however, no one will argue that all marriages enjoy relationship fully. Relating starts with taking initiative or responding to initiative but it cannot be continually repeated. Further, there may be a working relationship with or without emotional attachments. Teacher-student relationships, parent-child relationships, boss-subordinate relationships, master-slave relationships and so on have varying senses of intimacy, stability and continuation.

Relationship need not be steady and static, and as we notice in the lives of people it is perplexing and even bewildering. It may tread a slippery path while holding a very precious liquid in a vulnerable vessel. It may have to be like a candle in a storm. These and similar analogies have been used to define the nature of love and its susceptibility. The most sensitive and sensible application could be marital relationships. It is both fascinating and frustrating to watch the ways in which such relationships are forged and then broken. The chorus of 'I love you most' can turn to 'I hate you most.' There is no method that guarantees avoiding such tragedies. For example, in the case of arranged marriages (different from forced marriages), two persons work hard to understand one another, explore the depths of love together and on the whole live happily. Divorce is very rare, though many may live in misery or suffer in silence. Marriages of love, involving choice and a process of testing and familiarisation of the waters, seem to be breaking as if they were too brittle. Children are the worst victims of broken families although their material needs and protection may be assured. Without generalisation and further investigation into specific cases we can conclude that in any relationship, particularly marriage, the partners need to work hard to make it succeed and to lead a happy life even if they repeat exaggerated proclamations like 'We have enjoyed every minute!' This could be applied to interreligious relationship as well.

Generosity of the Spirit

Relationship may travel smoothly if basically there is generosity of the spirit. Those who believe in God as some sort of a person may point out his/her initiating grace and unfailing love. There are devotional traditions which extol God's grace and love that manifest themselves in nature and in human relations. Manikkavacakar, a Saiva devotee-saint-teacher, says that Lord Siva took all the colours of the nature upon his body. The Vaishnava teacher Ramanuja compares the brightness of the gracious God to that of a thousand suns. The Hebrew psalmist sings, 'The heavens declare the glory of God; the skies proclaim the work of his hands.' Jesus pointed out that the heavenly Father provides sunlight and rain to all whether they are righteous or wicked. His apostles declared that God is the source of all light, life and goodness. The Qur'an starts every chapter in the name of Allah, the most merciful and all compassionate. The operation of divine grace in Sikhism is not conceived differently. It is wonderful to reflect that God does not withdraw oxygen and other resources for life from those humans who may be wicked. God's generosity of the spirit is ready to give a holy kiss even to those who deny his existence!

If God is generous, gracious, compassionate and loving, why have there been hatred, atrocities and wars in the name of God? In every part of the world the earth is profaned by the shedding of innocent blood. Who will make it holy again and by what means? It is easier to justify what each religious community has done than to come together to find a common solution with generosity of the spirit. Orchestrated accusations and counter-accusations complicate issues beyond a stage of no return or a search for the truth. The famous Upanishadic prayer 'Lead me from untruth to truth...' may be a common mantra to be owned by all religious persons. Complications might lead to both ignorance and cynicism. To challenge this position, I would stress two facts. First, every religious tradition with a vision, tradition and willingness to experiment should apply generosity of the spirit in their own community. The Abrahamic traditions have a strong sense of being bound by a covenant and its associated commandments in order to build up a model community based on equality, justice, modesty, love and sharing. Though the other traditions may not have a mandate of this type, they have enough resources of spiritual edification and moral teaching to experiment with a similar community and principles. Sincere effort is the only test of the generosity of the spirit. Second, in a multi-religious community, demonstrating the same spirit in concrete ways shows experiment with truth. If we are not able to come together to do this, we can be sure that we have a long way to grasp our own religious visions and mobilise the resources for common good and realising our humanity. Remember, we live in a 'post-truth era', and for many truth does not go beyond a set of drinks, food, gambling and gossip. Only in the above way can religious communities become fascinating.

Dialogue and Relationship

Dialogue means two persons conversing, and in the discussions its meaning is extended to cover more than two persons conversing and debating. Dialogue stands for a programme as well, to organise conferences and consultations, action camps and publications including guidelines on interreligious dialogue. But does dialogue automatically presuppose a definite relationship or relationships between participants? Then the attitudinal principles of dialogue might be proposed. How do we want to see these principles leading to forge a relationship, especially an interreligious relationship? Persons of different religions coming together cannot be said to be forming a relationship. True dialogue cannot be casual but purposeful. Stanley Samartha (1920-2001), a South Indian theologian and pioneer of interreligious dialogue in the ecumenical movement through the WCC, defines:

> Dialogue is a mood, a spirit, an attitude of love and respect towards neighbours of other faiths. It regards partners as persons, not as statistics. Understood and practised as an intentional life-style, it goes far beyond a sterile co-existence or uncritical friendliness. It does not avoid controversies; it recognizes difficulties in relationships as well. It is not a gathering of porcupines; neither is it a get-together of jellyfish. Sensitively understood, it helps people not to disfigure the image of their neighbours of other faiths ...In multi-religious societies dialogue cannot be just the activity of a few interested individuals. It can only be 'dialogue in community'...communities of concerned people (must be) ready to take risk, to move beyond safe boundaries, to replace old particularities with new profiles.[1]

In this profound definition Samartha stresses more the emotional attitude, the dialogue of life and efforts to be able to change when convinced. It is not casual like the coming together of jellyfish, nor a gathering of porcupines in an agitative mood. It recognizes the importance of good relationships in community as well as difficulties in the experiencing the same. Samartha is very realistic in recognizing criticism and controversy, which are openly

---

[1] Samartha, *Courage for Dialogue*, Geneva: WCC, 1981, 100.

acknowledged in today's world and today's India. Hence much about dialogue remains shallow and superficial.

Dialogue presupposes a good relationship and atmosphere. Otherwise interreligious dialogue may turn to interreligious silence or noise. Rightly understood, dialogue is one of the greatest arts of communication. Speaking and listening proceed in right proportion in this communication. Abrupt interruptions upset the speaker and confuse the listener. By this irresponsible talk we can imagine how many millions of words are wasted even in a small community every day. Moreover, not merely incidental conversation but sustained dialogue builds up and matures relationship and makes the communication greater and greater. Being truthful is a cardinal virtue of this communication and it keeps relationship in purity.

Obviously, a dialogical society is a healthy one and it contributes to a healthy culture too. Introversion and insularity cause the formation of an internal volcano and it may well be that such people carry a few volcanoes which may end in mental outbursts. In certain parts of the modern world, there may be neighbourhoods but not necessarily neighbourliness. Professional counselling often takes the form of just listening, which is expensive. Thus, relationship cannot be a programme but must be natural and liberating. Interreligious relationship is all the more liberating, liberating us from ignorance about people of other religions. Racial prejudice is a disease of the mind because there is no ability to understand that it is no one's choice to be born in a particular race, skin colour and culture.

Gathering Model

The first World Parliament of Religions, held in the city of Chicago as part of the World Columbian Exposition in 1893, was the greatest hallmark of interreligious relationship. With about seven hundred participants it lasted for sixteen days (11-27 September) and introduced great figures from the major religious traditions of East and West. The Unitarians who were committed to forging interreligious relationship were in the forefront of organization of the Parliament. There were opportunities for speakers to proclaim the greatness of their respective religions. Most remarkable was the presence and speech of Swami Vivekananda, a Hindu reformer. His opening line of speech, 'Sisters and brothers of America', was greeted by a three-minute standing ovation from the audience. Pointing out sectarianism, bigotry and fanaticism, Vivekananda proudly announced that he represented a religion (Hinduism) which stood for deep spirituality, tolerance, unity and harmony. The impression he made not only on the audience but also on the whole world made him a self-acclaimed missionary of Neo-Vedanta, winning disciples in the West and mobilizing material resources for his Ramakrishna Mission.

For a century the fervour of the above may have been simmering but nonetheless had an effect on thinking minds. In 1988, the Council for a Parliament of the World's Religions (CPWR) was organized and their first event was the centenary celebration of the World Parliament in 1993. There were conferences and celebrations all over the world. In Chicago itself 8,000 people gathered for celebration and to explore the present conditions of religions. Subsequently, CPWR decided to organize periodic Parliaments and they included the one held in Cape Town, South Africa (1999), Barcelona, Spain (2004), Melbourne, Australia (2009), Salt Lake City, USA (2015), Toronto, Canada (2018).

How can we assess the effect of such world gatherings from the viewpoint of interreligious relationship? An authentic answer requires specialist research. No doubt, in spite of the milling around of about 9,000 people there were introductions, new acquaintances, sharing of knowledge and experience; what we do not know is whether there were friendships formed which led to lasting relationships and sustained dialogue. From the recorded speeches one notices stress on the equality and unity of religions. Perhaps the mission-minded Protestant Christians had to bear most of the beatings for their exclusive claims and the fundamentalists among them. Often exclusive claims in terms of a unique vision of God and life but in humility were not distinguished. Moreover, not only Swami Vivekananda, also other individuals and groups appeared in spectacular costumes. In some cases, they appeared to be a display of colours and fashions. For example, in Cape Town an aeroplane load of women from Japan in exotic uniforms landed and performed their distinctive spiritual practice and flew away without relating to others or being accessible to be related. At the same time, recent Parliaments have taken social issues such as HIV, projecting the best of all cultures. Further, new movements and organizations such as the International Association for Religious Freedom, the World Congress of Faiths, the Temple of Understanding, the World Fellowship of Faiths, World Thanksgiving, the World Inter-faith Association, the World Conference on Religion and Peace, and several networks such as the World Alliance of Inter-faith Organisations (USA) which organises world and regional conferences.

Conference and Consultation

In recent decades interreligious conferences and consultations have drawn the attention of the press and people. The above organisations organised several conferences and consultations, and participants have been drawn from different religious communities. It has been complained that many of them were not official representatives but managed to get invitation and entry. Journals and magazines report the proceedings and outcomes. Again, it is not clear that participants have related to others with openness and maintained further contacts, nor that on their return they advocate for good interreligious relationship among their religious communities.

As far as discussions on interreligious relationship are concerned within a religious tradition, Christianity excels others. Traditionally, Protestant Christian missions had the sole mandate of preaching the gospel and converting others into the church. However, long missionary encounters with world religions led to a new attitude and approach based on 'justice, courtesy and love'. This was reflected in the discussions in the first World Missionary Conference held in Edinburgh in 1910. The report of the Commission IV came out in the form of a book entitled *The Missionary Message in Relation to Non-Christian Religions*. However, though there was a change of tone and advocacy for a new approach, there was no compromise on the indispensable duty of every Christian to preach the gospel. Subsequent decades saw further attestation of this stand with new arguments for the uniqueness of Christianity or revelation in Christ, although there were voices for radical restatement of the gospel and reassessment of the validity of other religions. This trend hit the climax when the sub-unit on Dialogue with People of Other Faiths and Ideologies was established in the WCC in 1971 with Stanley Samartha as founder director. This sub-unit has taken different shapes, names and emphases, but its influence on the thinking and other programme units has been considerable. It has been controversial too. In the fifth General Assembly of the WCC in Nairobi in Kenya in 1975, for the first time, five representatives from other religions attended as guests and the issue of interreligious relation was openly discussed. The controversy led to organising a further conference in Chiang Mai, Thailand, in 1977 in order to clarify issues and prepare guidelines. Since then several conferences and consultations have been held and publications produced. Most participants have had already some relationship with members of other religious communities and the conference/consultation experience for them further informed them and encouraged them to enlighten their fellow Christians about proper relationship with their neighbours of other religions.

Guidelines and other Literature

The above-mentioned consultation held in Chiang Mai, Thailand, in 1977, on the theme 'Dialogue in Community', resulted in a set of *Guidelines on Dialogue with People of Living Faiths and Ideologies* published by the WCC in 1979. The booklet was widely circulated and translated into many languages. Drawing on relevant insights from the Bible, the 'Guidelines' in Part One define human community as a community of communities with relationships, shared values, the building of nations, and the maintenance of harmony. It mentions the Christian affirmation of God's love for all people, the rich variety of cultures and the need for mobilizing religious and ideological resources for common good. Then the unique nature of the Christian community or Church is discussed. It is recognized that Christians share life and many values with other communities, themselves being varied. There is the universal appeal of the Gospel which has transformed communities, the need for unity among Christians, the authority of the Bible, the unavoidable tension between Christian communities and other human communities, and our continued participation in God's mission. These concerns form Part One of the 'Guidelines'.

Part Two first points out the reasons for dialogue which include the growing multifaith and multi-cultural milieus that call for a new life-style, clear and personal communication and an authentic expression of love, thus witnessing to Christ. Then it moves on to focusing on the theological significance of people of other faiths and ideologies. Christians should approach this with repentance for wrong doing in the past, with humility about our limited self-understanding, with the joy of being disciples of Jesus, and with a sense of the need for a new approach with integrity and openness. Further, a number of questions are raised about the relationship between God's universal presence and action, and the special experience of Christians in Christ. The idea of syncretism is explained, the confusion exposed and tendencies to deviation recognized.

Part Three of the 'Guidelines' contains recommendations to Churches. They are arranged under three sub-headings: learning and understanding in dialogue, sharing and living together in dialogue, and planning for dialogue. A Christian initiative for interfaith dialogue which then has to be planned together, clear self-definition in partnership with others, educational efforts to understand what others believe, sharing fully in community life while being loyal to their respective visions and commitments, sharing in celebrations, and careful planning with selection of suitable delegates for interfaith meetings at different levels, are the most important points of recommendation.

The WCC Guidelines on Dialogue inspired Churches around the world to produce guidelines in the same or slightly different lines to suit their contexts. Churches in the United Kingdom excel in the production of such guidelines and study materials. They can very well fill a sizeable book-shelf and provide sufficient source materials for a postgraduate research project. The sub-unit on Dialogue which has gone through different names and locations in the changing WCC structures too continued further exploration into the theological and practical issues of interfaith dialogue. It has influenced discussions on mission and evangelism within the WCC, particularly through its strongest department, the Commission on World Mission and Evangelism. Consequently, no mission statement has come out without some considerable reference to people of other faiths and interfaith dialogue. The contribution and influence of Wesley Ariarajah, a junior colleague of Samartha, who later succeeded him as the Director of the sub-unit, is evident both explicitly and implicitly. This is besides his lectures and publications which have fired the imagination of so many theologians and ministers, including the writer of this article.

'Taking stock of 30 years of dialogue and revisiting the 1979 Guidelines' (*Current Dialogue*, No. 40, 2000, 16-21) is a document that updates the concerns of interfaith relations and dialogue. It stresses the fact of recent conflicts which have been presented as caused by religions while in actual fact religion is used as a cover and excuse for the pursuits of vested interests. It also touches the question of the uneven power relations which affect genuine and open dialogue between people. It should also be pointed out that since the Second Vatican Council (1962-65) the Roman Catholic Church has been showing great interest in interreligious dialogue. The staff of the Pontifical Secretariat for interreligious relations and their counterparts in WCC have initiated joint study programmes on issues such as interreligious marriage and interreligious prayer, and have issued joint statements on good interreligious relations in the context of conflict or potential conflict situations. The exploration continues in various different forms.

India presents a unique situation. Nearly two thousand years of Christian presence, more than five hundred years of Catholic mission and three hundred years of Protestant mission with costly resources expended for communication and social service have resulted in a tiny minority of about 2.5 percent Christians. They live along with about 82 percent 'Hindus', 12 percent Muslims, 2 percent Sikhs and with Buddhists, Jains, Parsees and Jews, fewer in number. The Indian sub-continent has been the cradle of some of the major world faiths such as Buddhism, Jainism, Hinduism and Sikhism. Though Islam and Christianity were brought from outside, over the centuries they have consciously and unconsciously inherited many Indian colours and characteristics. The Indian situation is a point of reference in ecumenical discussions on interreligious dialogue. Indian Christian theologians such as A.J. Appasamy, P.D. Devanandan, J.R. Chandran, M.M. Thomas and S.J. Samartha have made valuable contributions to these discussions. However, nothing can be of greater irony than that Indian churches do not want to be affected by these discussions. Conservatism, strangely combined with fundamentalist revival, appears to rule and there is much apathy or indifference to interreligious dialogue; it is even taken as a threat to Christian commitment to mission. A few isolated attempts have been made, mainly in institutions outside the churches. I have made an attempt to produce a set of Guidelines for the Indian context.[2] They include the following: shared national identity, shared values, shared religiosity and resources, what Christians hold as distinctive, recommendations for initiating interreligious dialogue, and conclusion. On the whole, guidelines certainly help the confused and wavering to have a grasp of the basic issues involved. However, we have to ask the question to what extent they have been read and appropriated by Christians and whether in turn they have tried to forge relationships with their neighbours of other religion. An empirical study will be greatly valuable.

Friendship, the Highest Form of Relationship

If we reflect deeply, it is obvious that friendship is the greatest of relationships. Even relationships such as husband-wife, parent-child, teacher-student and sister-sister/brother may develop into an overarching friendship. Then it should follow that interreligious friendship is a possibility.

Then, what is friendship? One may think that it is an unnecessary question as friendship is too obvious. Let us consider a few cases of using the word friendship: 'I had a friend forty years ago.'

---

[2] I. Selvanayagam, "Guidelines for Christians on Interfaith Dialogue in India: Some Notes" in *Theology Beyond Neutrality: Essays to Honour Wesley Ariarajah*, ed. by Marshal Fernando and Robert Crusz, Colombo: Ecumenical Institute, 2011, 103-116; *NCC Review*, CXXX1/11, Dec. 2011, 38-56.

'She is my closest friend.' 'He is a good friend.' If you press further, some may very well say 'I know them.' Still pressed further the answer may be 'We met a few times' or 'I met him in a conference.' Can such a casual acquaintance be called friendship? Dictionaries give the meaning of friendship as the relationship between friends and friendly disposition; a friend being one with whom another enjoys mutual affection and regard; one who can be sympathetic and empathetic, and a helper or patron; one who stands on our side. A speaker addressing her audience 'dear friends' is formal. The related adjective 'friendly' is meant as well-disposed, kindly, being ready to approve, convenient to use, accessible to help and doing something (e.g. playing a match) for enjoyment and bonding relationship (as opposed to professional or commercial). We hear of friendly societies such as the Friends of the Earth and even dialogue groups such as the Religious Friends Circle (e.g. in TTS, Madurai). However, it is difficult to define friendship.

Jesus was unique in defining friendship. Towards the end of his life on earth he told his disciples:

> My command is this: love each other as I have loved you. Greater love has no one than this: to lay down one's life for one's friends. You are my friends if you do what I command. I no longer call you servants, because a servant does not know his master's business. Instead, I have called you friends, for everything that I learned from my Father I have made known to you (John 15: 12-15).

Essentially, friendship is defined by intimate love, transparency and being prepared to lay down life. It looks an impossible ideal, but Jesus kept it effortlessly as is evident in his calling 'friend' his estranged disciple Judas who had just betrayed him with a kiss. It seems that for Jesus friendship was not casual, sentimental and occasional. Obeying his command in all instances of life alone expresses true love and friendship. Interreligious friendship can be formed, and already we know real stories, perhaps more among the poor and the labourers. Even if it remains an ideal there is no reason not to move towards it.

Commitment and Openness

Commitment and openness are two indispensable eyes. It is no wonder that the publication of a doctoral dissertation on the interreligious dialogue and theology of religions in the work of Stanley Samartha (1920-2001) by a European scholar was titled *Commitment and Openness.*[3] Samartha was fully aware that he was the descendent of converts to Christianity from one of the Hindu religious traditions in South India. He committed to ministry at a young age and was ordained a presbyter of the Church of South India. His contribution to theological education and ministerial training in India was considerable. Perhaps, more significant was his contribution to the ministry of interreligious dialogue in the ecumenical movement, as we have already noted. He continued to emphasise in his writings that real dialogue can take place only where there is commitment.

For Samartha, talking about people of other faiths or initiating interfaith dialogue was not part of his position in a university department, nor as being part of a scholarly group who did not bother about their own religious commitment. Moving beyond purposeless gatherings and wish-washy platitudes and superficial gestures of respect, he encouraged partners in dialogue to move on taking efforts to understand each other's faith and seeking avenues of interreligious cooperation with proximate goals in the common human life in concrete contexts.

Samartha engaged in dialogue with Hindu thinkers and analysed their responses to the 'unbound Christ'. He had found no reason to respond to the revivalist Hindu call to go back to the mother religion. He advocated for those engaged in dialogue to have their own theological backbones. At one level he perceived religions representing different responses to the Mystery but yet at another level he warned against 'rudderless boats in the waters of relativism'. He tried through bible studies and sermons to motivate Christians to muster 'courage for dialogue'.

---

[3] Eeuwout Klootwijk, Zoetermeer: Uitgeverij Boekencentrum B.V., 1992.

Respect with Responsibility

Respect for different faiths and ideologies is regarded as a virtue of a civilised life and fruit of enlightenment as understood in the western world. Respect for freedom was part of it. People have worshipped the goddess of freedom along with the goddess of reason. But today even in the affluent world people teach about healthy diet and responsible enjoyment for the health of the society and nation.

Similarly, when we ask for respect for religions we need to emphasise commitment and responsibility. We may affirm the equality of all religions in terms of communities' identity and belief. But that does not mean that all the beliefs and practices, irrespective of their contribution to personal health and community health, should be respected. Narrow forms of cohesion and coherence with segregation and division may be a necessary corollary to some faith traditions. Equality of women, disabled and children may be scientifically untenable for some believers. Stratification of society, hierarchy of communities and untouchability may be tolerated if not perpetuated because of their connection with religious visions and traditions. The immoral invasion of a country and illegal war may be justified by fascist groups who use their religion as support. Should we respect such things in a multi-religious society? Only interreligious friendship provides a safe space and solid outcome when we discuss these issues.

Arun Gandhi, a grandson of Mahatma Gandhi, and an executive member ofThe Interfaith Alliance, in his Gandhi's birthday message through the internet (2 Oct '07) mentions the following:

> Mahatma also pointed out: 'Love is the subtlest force in the world.' He said we need to respect people who may be different, and this requires much more of us than merely tolerating people's differences. With 'tolerance,' you could believe you don't need to like or even talk to the other person – the stranger, the foreigner, and the 'infidel'– and we all lose. The point is: showing respect requires much more effort, more humility and more understanding.

> Respect only comes about when we learn more about one another – and this is one of the most important functions of The Interfaith Alliance – as it pulls together leaders and adherents from more than over 50 different faith traditions, for open dialogue and respectful cooperation.

Those who take Gandhi as an inspiration for interreligious harmony and dialogue hardly take into account his plea for respect and tolerance with genuine commitment to understand the other and abolish evils such as poverty and untouchability. Those who do not attach them to the effect of their religion, Gandhi would ask them to show their open commitment to denounce them and abolish them.

Religious Life and Commitment

Religious nominalism is one of the greatest hurdles for interreligious dialogue. When charismatic leaders take religion into their hands and use it for political gains they cannot become models of committed life to religious vision and openness to the vision of others. The painful partition of the subcontinent into India and Pakistan in 1947, which led to the gruesome mass murder of more than a million people, sent mixed signals as far as religious commitment was concerned. It is said that Mohammed Ali Jinnah, the champion of the Pakistan movement, was not a practising Muslim and was very secularised in his life-style. Jawaharlal Nehru was an avowed agnostic who wanted to build modern temples of dams, industries and democracy. Gandhi continued to be a devotee of Ram, the divine hero and one of the incarnations of Vishnu, but explained the reign of Ram as identical with the reign of God the chief characteristics of which are love, justice, equality, tolerance and so on. But Ambedkar, the champion of Dalit liberation with reference to mythological stories saw Ram as the oppressor of the low caste people and the outcaste Dalits.

In a rather hurried act of compromise, India continued to be Hindu-Muslim along with the minorities of Christians, Sikhs and others. And the Ashokan wheel found a place in the Indian logo which symbolised equal respect for all religions. Ironically, Gautama Buddha, the fierce critic of Brahmanic religion, had been absorbed into the system as one of the avatars of Vishnu, while Ambedkar and his thousands of followers left the Hindu fold and became Buddhists, thus giving life to the neo-Buddhist movement in India. At the same time, there are Hindus who take Buddhism and Jainism (another protest movement along with Buddhism) as sub-sects of Hinduism which is not agreed by most Buddhists and Jains. In such a context, how do we understand respect and commitment? Again, the prerequisite interreligious friendship is the answer.

There may be people who in a secular climate do not express their religious commitment openly and publicly. There may be philosophers and historians of religion in the phenomenological study. There may be agnostics, methodological and personal. There may be humanists who are concerned about the utility value of interreligious dialogue for communal harmony and interreligious collaboration on issues of common welfare. A stable relationship alone would promise a healthy, sustained and meaningful dialogue. Interreligious relationship may be vital to have meaningful dialogue with non-religious, irreligious or anti-religious. One can even say that such exercise will help to bring out the inner aspirations and to grow in the civility of life. The following chapters will illustrate the dynamics and diverse spheres of interreligious relationship.

Chapter 2

Interreligious Education

Learning Together

In true and serious relationship there is an eagerness to know the other. There are unlimited opportunities to know and explore together. The participants in such relationship may soon realize how shallow and superficial their knowledge of one another has been. This is true of not only general friendship and familiar bonds but also interreligious relationship. Knowing the beliefs, practices and experiences of other religious people may look demanding and unsettling. But if the relationship is lively, knowing becomes easy, even exciting. Basic is the discovery that the other is different and that their religiosity and religious life are different. What is frustratingly common is that if one takes the position that all religions are essentially the same, then there is no urge to learn and know. Even at that level there are opportunities to explore together what is that essence and how it manifests in different religions. It is a dictum that fear of knowing the other and their religion is a sign of lacking self-understanding of one's own religion and uncertainty about its uniqueness.

Originally it was in the context of Christian mission that the need of knowing other religions was felt. However, the knowing was expressly in order to know the 'enemy camp' and win. But two problems were encountered. First, study of other religions and their scriptures in their own language proved to be limited. As far as the Hindu religious traditions are concerned, for example, scholars of Oriental studies focused on the Sanskrit literature which was thought to be the master narrative of Hinduism. It was realized, in due course, that numerous literatures were in the vernacular, both in sectarian traditions and popular cults. Also, it was realized that there were oral traditions in remote villages. In recent years some of them have been studied with curiosity and interest in cultural systems, mainly by western scholars. The spirit of 'knowing the enemy to invade' continues among Christian enthusiasts who spoil the possibilities of discovering together with sympathy and empathy.

Second, without boasting one may observe that Christian engagement in the study of other religions has been not matched by Hindu, Buddhist, Jaina, Islamic and Sikh traditions. In Christian theological education and ministerial training, the study of other religions is ever moving to greater heights. One can imagine the position of those who are engaged in the study being frustrated by lack of study of other religions while many of their fellow Christians suspect their commitment. Moreover, from the experience of interreligious relationship and dialogue, we have come to the realization that the best form of interreligious study is collective exploration with openness into the spiritual wells of religious traditions. However, we seem to have a long journey to go to achieve it. Illiteracy, irreligionists and religious nominalism add to the slow progress. With this backdrop, this chapter traces important early attempts and the milestones in this journey, again from the Christian side. The subject continues to be dealt with from different angles.

A Significant Consultation

'Theological Education and Ministerial Formation' was the title of a consultation in Kuala Lumpur in 1985, jointly organised by the Programme on Theological Education and the Dialogue Sub-unit of the World Council of Churches. It was an attempt to explore issues involved in training ministers in a multifaith context. 'The participants came from fourteen nations and eighteen theological schools. It was the first time so wide a range of theological educators had come together to examine the implications of interreligious dialogue for their work.' A number of questions were raised. For example, if genuine theology arises out of reflection within a given context, can theological teachers and students ignore their religious and spiritual environment? Does not this environment call for a new attitude on the part of Christians to their neighbours of other faiths? How can both theological educators and students equip themselves to respond to the challenges posed by the resurgence of some traditional religions particularly in Asia? How can we encourage and develop an Asian reading of the scriptures which is fundamental to the teaching of theology in Asia and Asian theology itself? What is the purpose of teaching and learning religions in a ministerial training institution? Various issues involved in ministerial formation in a multifaith milieu were identified, and experiences and experiments of various ministerial training institutions in Asia were shared. The 'summary of the general recommendations' include the following:

The reality of religious pluralism must be recognised. Teachers of biblical subjects, as well as of the history of doctrine and church history, must be encouraged to develop non-exclusive hermeneutics of both the Bible and Tradition. A thorough examination of the motivation for the teaching of religion is required. Is it missiological? Apologetic? Is it done in a way which is conducive to good interreligious relations?

> The teaching of religion must be integrated with the teaching of the theology of world religions and the theology of mission.
>
> The teaching of the theology of mission must undergird the teaching of both evangelism and dialogue, and that theology of mission must take into consideration the goals of community building, shalom, justice and liberation.
>
> Theological teachers, just as much as ministers of the church already engaged in mission and pastoral care, need

> a continuing programme of training to enable them to respond constructively to religious pluralism.[4]

There were 'Some practical suggestions' made, and they included;

> Textbooks used in seminaries should be carefully examined in the light of the concern of interreligious dialogue. Wherever possible, textbooks on other religions should be written by adherents of those religions. New theological textbooks need to be developed.
>
> New methods, such as team teaching, need to be explored in order to ensure an integrated approach among teachers of different theological disciplines. Team teaching involving members of other religious traditions is also important.
>
> Studies should be developed of the image of Christianity and Christian communities that is projected among our neighbours of other faiths and religious communities. In particular, there should be studies on how the central themes and doctrines of Christianity have been understood by people of other faiths.
>
> ...a network [should] be set up of those who are active in teaching world religions in theological seminaries. The purpose would be to exchange resources, information, publications, teaching materials, particular course syllabi and reading lists.[5]

Some of the reflections shared in this consultation we will mention later on. It should be noted, however, that on the whole the consultation reflected more a 'brain storming' than sessions developing clear guidelines and arranging for their implementation. Also, it was difficult to develop a consistent pattern as theological

---

[4] *Ministerial Formation in a Multi-Faith Milieu - Implications of Interfaith Dialogue for Theological Education*, ed. by S. Amirtham and W. Ariarajah, Geneva: WCC, 1986, 17f.

[5] Ibid., 18f.

institutions in Asia and other continents have been operating with different structures and affiliations. It would be a worthwhile study to gather information and analyse the contents of subjects on other religions taught in ministerial training institutions worldwide. The scope of this chapter is rather limited and it will present the cases of India and Britain and end with a discussion on the theological and missiological issues in approaching the study of other religions.

The Study of Religions in India

Some inter-religious and inter-cultural institutes based in Bangalore jointly organised a consultation in 1967 to consider the position of the study of religion in the Indian universities. The Christian component was well represented not only by the Christian Institute for the Study of Religion and Society, which was one of the sponsors of this important consultation, but also by the participation of Christian scholars of religions such as Stanley Samartha, John Carman and Wilfred Cantwell Smith. Carman, the programme secretary, in his opening presentation observed:

> Up to the present, Indian Universities have generally not recognised Studies of Religion as a distinct field to be followed in a separate department. Some aspects of a few religions have been studied within some of the existing departments of the Faculties of Arts: Philosophy, History, Sociology, and the various languages, such as the Sanskrit, Arabic, Persian, Bengali and Tamil.[6]

The historical reason for the lack of a Department of Religious Studies, Carman continues to state, 'lies in the founding of modern Indian universities on the model of the "modern" and "secular" British University of the mid-nineteenth century, the University of London. But the choice of this model and its continuing influence is by no means an historical accident. The British Colonial rulers felt that it was appropriate to encourage and support such a secular

[6] J.B. Carman, "The Study of Religion in the Indian University", in *Study of Religion in Indian Universities - A Report of the Consultation held in Bangalore in September, 1967*, Bangalore: The Bangalore Press, 1969, 1.

University, for they were committed in principle to a policy of neutrality between India's many religious communities. Religious study was understood in Britain in the nineteenth century to be nothing else than the instruction of students in a particular tradition. As such, it could be tolerated and even somewhat encouraged in sectarian institutions under private auspices, but the University, directly supported by a religiously neutral government, could not allow such religious studies within its own portals.'[7] The appropriate places for such study were institutions run by particular religious communities - schools and colleges - but the level was basic and preliminary, and the spirit was apologetic. Particularly, the case in the Christian theological seminaries has been made subject to gradual reconsideration.

The British neutrality in the matter of religion affected considerably that clause of the Indian Constitution which deals with religious education, although the clause on freedom of religion can be taken as clashing with it. Religious instruction in the universities supported by the State is expressly prohibited by the Indian Constitution.[8] The irony is that while the study of Indian religions increasingly became popular in the West with often Indian scholars chairing the departments of 'Comparative Religion' as in the case of Radhakrishnan in Oxford, it has continuously been excluded from the Indian universities. Some leaders and thinkers are unhappy about this and even expressed a dilemma as reflected in the reports of some of the University Education Commissions. For example, the famous Kothari Commission (1965), takes up the question of the implications of a secularist policy by the State towards religion and religious education. It states:

> The adoption of a secularist policy means that in political, economic, and social matters, all citizens, irrespective of their religious faith, will enjoy equality of rights, that no religious community will be favoured or discriminated against, and that instruction in religious dogmas will not be provided in the State schools. But it is *not* an irreligious

[7] Ibid.

[8] See Ibid., 2.

> or anti-religious policy; it does *not* belittle the importance of religion as such. It gives to every citizen the fullest freedom of religious beliefs and worship. It is anxious to ensure good relations among different religious groups and to promote not only religious tolerance but also an active reverence for all religions.[9]

The desired 'good relations among different religious groups' is in fact not accompanied by any serious effort to understand one another's faith. And the 'active reverence' suggested is often demanded by those whose religious practices are ambiguous if not deplorable. This is true at all levels. Consequently, what is dominant is either a grave distortion and misrepresentation of the religion of others which causes communal tension, or the slogan of 'one Truth and many religions,' repeated by politicians and philosophers, which has contributed to the continuation of interreligious ignorance. In any case, later, while a few universities managed to establish a separate department of comparative religion, some others have been satisfied with running a course on moral or value education under existing departments like philosophy. Also, there has been increasing interest in establishing chairs on particular religions funded by the respective religious communities. There have been attempts to create novel programmes of bi-lateral studies. For instance, the Tamilnadu Theological Seminary, Madurai, started an MA in Saiva Siddhanta and Christian Theology in 1974 with affiliation to the local Madurai Kamaraj University, but in due course it became unpopular as the graduates could not establish their departmental identity when they were desperately seeking employment. Another example is the establishment in the 1990s of a new Department of Interreligious Relations in the same university. It too has dwindled. It is in this context we need to understand the place and pattern of the study of other religions in ministerial training colleges.

All the mainstream theological colleges and ministerial training institutions of the Protestant churches in India are affiliated to the Senate of Serampore College (University) based in a suburb of Kolkata. The College was founded by the Baptist missionaries Carey,

[9] Quoted, Ibid., 15.

Marshman and Ward in 1818. Further to the establishment of several schools, a Danish Royal Charter obtained by Marshman in 1827 qualified the College to confer degrees, and it became the first European type university in Asia. The Serampore College Prospectus of 1818, in its preamble, states that the college shall secure instruction in the Sanskrit language of all the native Christian youth admitted. It further stated:

> It shall secure their being further instructed in the various shastras of the hindoos and in the doctrines which form the basis of the Pauranic and Boudhist systems. They shall also be instructed in those which relate to Hindoo-Law.[10]

While Carey and his colleagues found the natives to be 'poor, barbarous, naked pagans and destitute of civilization and true religion', as the Prospectus mentions, they wanted the Christian youth 'to enjoy the highest literary advantages of their own country as fully as the highest castes among the Hindoos'. It is a long and exciting story that the Serampore missionaries made a valuable and lasting contribution to the study of Sanskrit and Bengali languages and socio-economic reformation, often in collaboration with Hindu reformers like Ram Mohan Roy. Part of the story was the controversy between the Serampore missionaries and Calcutta thinkers over their attitude to the Hindu religious traditions and Christian doctrines. This controversy provides many insights for those who consider mission in a multi-religious context and those committed to the ministry of interreligious dialogue. Our limited concern here is to see how the study of other religions has been part of theological education and ministerial training in India.

The missionary legacy of approaching and studying other religions inherited by the Senate of Serampore College (University), on the whole, may be said to be characterised by the following motives: scoring points for the supremacy of Christianity by showing the degrading and superstitious beliefs and practices, achieving a mastery of knowledge of the classics and philosophical traditions

[10] Quoted, K.P. Aleaz, *Dimensions of Indian Religion - Study, Experience and Interaction*, Calcutta: Punthi Pustak, 1995, 202.

in order to look respectable and acceptable before thinkers, and developing strategy for communicating the gospel to people of other faiths. Knowing the enemy camp in order to make strategic moves to attack and conquer, perhaps, is still the prime motive of most of those Christian ministers and evangelists who choose to study other religions. While the Senate makes provision in the curriculum for the study of religions and requires certain compulsory courses and standards, there is no way to guarantee a proper approach and attitude in its implementation. However, the genuine efforts of the Senate to develop a comprehensive and dialogical approach to the study of religions and produce scholars in the field are unquestionable. This is evident in the guidelines, revisions of the syllabi and consultations initiated by the Senate. Without daring to present a history of developments in this connection, we will point out the major concerns and programmes.

In the wake of an increasing number of theological schools including some sectarian groups seeking affiliation, the Senate of Serampore College appointed a commission to develop 'Evaluation Criteria for Affiliation – 1991.' The stated 'objectives of the institution' seeking affiliation should include:

> increasing sensitivity to cultural, religious and social dimensions in the country and their missiological implications;
>
> presenting the gospel in a religiously pluralistic context;
>
> deepening commitment to ministry through a proper understanding of one's faith in the context of the world.[11]

There are clear guidelines for those institutions offering degrees (BTh, BD, BRE, MTh) and diploma courses. The branch of Religions or 'Religions, Culture and Society' is given a place on a par with the other major branches. For instance, class hours (including guided learning hours) suggested for BTh Religions are 200 which is the same for Theology and Ethics, History of Christianity and Christian Ministry although the Old Testament and New Testament parts of

[11] 'Senate of Serampore College – Evaluation Criteria for Affiliation', 2.

the Bible get 350 hours and an optional extra 150. Incidentally, BTh has now been phased out, and in its place a new Integrated BD has been introduced. In the case of BD, hours for Bible are reduced to 300, and for History of Christianity and Religions to 100, but 'optionals' get 400 which include areas of Communication, Social Analysis and Inter-Disciplinary in which the multi-religious concern can be a component. (Consult the present division of clusters and the spread of courses.)

According to the revised curriculum of the Senate with effect from 1991, courses mentioned for BTh are: 'Outlines of major Religious Traditions in the Sub-Continent', 'Christians and People of Other Faiths', 'Modern Religious and Secular Movements and Trends in the Indian Sub-Continent', 'Study of Regional and Local Religious Traditions', 'Introduction to Indian Philosophy', of which the first three are required. For BD 'The Study of Major Religions of India in their Socio-Cultural Context', 'Detailed Study of Hinduism with Prescribed Texts', 'Renascent and Contemporary Movements in India' and 'Christian Response to People of Other Faiths' are required, and the optionals include 'Methodological Issues: Contemporary Approaches to the Study of Religion', 'Primal Religions in the Sub-Continent', 'Indian Philosophy', 'Sanskrit', and 'Cultural Anthropology'. The new degree programme of BCS (Bachelor of Christian Studies) requires the two courses of 'Study of Religious Traditions: Contemporary Approaches' and 'Religious Pluralism and Christian Witness'. The MTh programme which provided originally a pattern for other branches has general subjects like Methods or Approaches to the Study of Religion and the specialized areas of Hinduism, Islam or Buddhism in which exegetical study of prescribed texts of these traditions in their original language is built in. Besides, there is a doctoral programme (DTh) which includes preparatory studies in general methodology and a dissertation on a topic related to one of the above three religious traditions or interreligious dialogue. Since 1991 a number of reviews have been initiated and small amendments made.

In spite of all the above arrangements, study of religions in the context of ministerial formation is side-lined, lacks clear focus and method and remains isolated. Where there is a spirit of 'knowing the enemy' there is some enthusiasm. Otherwise, a respectful distance is maintained by experts of other disciplines in spite of all slogans of inter-disciplinary and integrated approaches. This is echoed by scholars of religions and social analysts of the programmes. For example, as early as 1980, Herbert Jai Singh, long-standing teacher of Religions, expressed his impression that a survey and analysis of Christian study of religions in India in the past would reveal the fact that this study had not been undertaken for its own sake, but to serve the apologetic purpose of evangelism. In his view this was true of missionary writings on other religions and of studies undertaken by some Indian Christian scholars. He did not want the study of religions to be a mere tool in the hands of Christian theologians and emphasised the need 'to accept the History of Religions as a discipline in its own right and give it an independent status of its own, distinguishing it clearly from apologetics.'[12] The concern of Singh who had special studies in Chicago in the company of scholars like Mircea Eliade is understandable. Nevertheless, what he failed to clarify was the exact purpose of studying religions by the ministers of a minority church feeling sandwiched between the majority of Hindus of an immense variety of beliefs and practices ranging from blood sacrifices to transcendental meditation with a host of philosophers, politicians and illiterate masses joining in the chorus of 'one truth and many religions' on the one hand, and Muslims with a claim of new revelation with an appeal to correct the Christian understanding of Jesus on the other. As a presbyter of the Church of North India he knew the tremendous influence of popular forms of Hinduism on Indian Christians who appeared with a cloak borrowed from the West. At the same time, his own suggestion is questionable. For example, was he advocating picking up a piece of information about people of other religions for the increase of human knowledge or simply following the Western pattern of comparative religion with a claim of methodological agnosticism which led to a theological agnosticism and indifference to mission and which, to a considerable extent, has been the reason for church decline in the West?

---

[12] See H. J. Singh, "Teaching of Religions in the Indian Context", *The Indian Journal of Theology*, 29/3&4, July-December., 1980, 150-153.

The Senate of Serampore College (University) appointed a team of social scientists to study and analyse the content of the courses of its curriculum and the report was available in 1985 although it could not be carried out with thoroughness and depth as had been intended originally. Hunter Mabry, the co-ordinator of the team, observed:

> For the Senate, History of Christianity, and Religion and Philosophy, receive the least emphasis, with prescribed courses in each constituting only 8 per cent of the total required hours...There is considerable variation in attention given to Religion and Philosophy with prescribed hours in this branch constituting from 5 to 21 per cent of total class hours for the BD programme...At the same time, some colleges give the greatest emphasis to these branches. No rationale was provided for these opposite patterns.[13]

Presumably, the exceptional 'some colleges' include TTS, Madurai and UTC, Bangalore where, apart from fulfilling the requirements of the Senate, creative courses are run with programmes of practical exposure. Further, Jai Singh who analysed the content of 'Religions' observed varying styles, stated objectives, titles, focus and approach adopted by different colleges. Consistent, however, was attention given to all the major religious traditions of India with special study of at least one which, in most cases, was Hinduism. While 'the Senate seeks through this course to help students in communicating the gospel to people of other faiths in a meaningful way', he observes, 'while one college seeks to enter into fruitful dialogue with Hindus, another college seeks to relate the study of Hinduism to prevalent social and political conditions – although it is not specified what this means.' As for the methodology, he states:

> It is difficult to say much about any *dominant* assumptions in *methodology*. Some colleges appear to follow a phenomenological or philosophical or historical approach, others to use some combination of these, including also

[13] H. Mabry, "Content Analysis of Theological Curricula", *Religion and Society*, XII/3, September, 1985, 10f.

> comparative, sociological and /or theological approaches. The methodological assumptions will depend upon which of these approach(es) is/are chosen.[14]

It is true that in different ways the above variety is applicable to other branches of study also, and it is very difficult for the Senate to ensure consistency and standard as the colleges are spread all over the vast country. There is no dearth of efforts, however, to inculcate a common understanding in all the member colleges of what is known as the 'Serampore family'.

'Theological Education in the Indian Context of Development' was the theme of the triennial national theological teachers' conference held in 1981 at Mangalore. Development was perceived to be one of the major concerns of the theological colleges in India, 'a country where nearly two thirds of the population are said to be either at the border or below the poverty line.' The pluralistic religious context of the country was given due attention since it is impossible to develop the country with the resources and inspiration of only one religious community. Godwin Singh who reflected on this fact emphasised that beyond fulfilling the academic requirements, every student should be motivated to enter into fruitful dialogue with people of other religions, thereby showing dialogue as an authentic life style grounded on the divine incarnation in Christ and him being the unifying centre of all positive values here and at the end of time. His plea for a shift in the motive of studying other religions extended to cover a new openness to see the work of the Spirit beyond the boundaries of the Christian church. In his words,

> So far theological education studied other religious systems in order to be able to criticise or refute them. But now it must provide an environment for dialogue believing that Christian mission and faithfulness to the Gospel imply a respect for men of all faiths. Dialogue is not an academic discussion, but it is an adventure into the experience of dialogue itself. While scholarly competence and academic detachment are certainly required, emphasis is not on

---

[14] H.J. Singh, Op.cit., 76.

> the concept of dialogue but on the actual engagement in dialogue itself. Our faith lived in a pluralistic religious context must emphasise the economy of the Holy Spirit through the theology of dialogue, i.e., Christ's presence beyond the boundaries of Christian history. The economy of the salvific Christ event cannot be understood apart from the economy of the Spirit which is everywhere present filling all things. The Christian understanding of creation as an act of grace and of God's love extending to the whole mankind is already an adequate basis on which to engage in dialogue.[15]

Such theological vision, for Singh, must find expression not only in our relation to people of other faiths in building up and developing our nation, but also as praxis-oriented theological training in which encounter with people of other faiths can inform a creative reflection and motivate us for collective action. How to integrate these concerns and ensure implementation is a continuing concern of the Senate.

The Board for Theological Education of the Senate of Serampore College (University) organised a series of consultations for both teachers of Religions and teachers of other disciplines during 1988-1990. One outcome of these meetings was a document entitled *Syllabus: Recommended for Use in Connection with the Bachelor of Divinity Degree Course of Study* (1991). With regard to the methodological issues relating to the branch on 'Religion and Society' it states:

In the contemporary approaches to the study of Religion the following points can be mooted:

> (a) Majority of present day scholars are convinced about the polymethodic nature of the study of religions. (b) Each of the different approaches has been given varying shades of definition and each approach is undergoing developments.

[15] G.R. Singh, "Theological Education in the Context of Pluralistic Religious Society", in *Theological Education and Development*, ed. by G. Robinson, H. Wilson and C. Duraisingh, Bangalore: The Association of Theological Teachers in India, 1984, 40f.

> (c) To meet the challenge of formulating an Indian methodology or methodologies in the study of religion is very essential. It is observed that religion and philosophy are inseparably related in the study of Hinduism; suggested that sociological and social anthropological approaches as well as philosophical approaches together should contribute to an integral approach to the study of religion.[16]

The impact of teachers of religions like K.P. Aleaz whose main orientation is to the philosophical traditions of India can be easily seen in the discussions that resulted in this statement. His own statements betray this. For instance, the section on 'methodological issues in the study of religion' in one of his recent books ends with the words: 'We are envisaging a dialogical sociological approach, a dialogical social anthropological approach, a dialogical philosophical approach, etc., in the study of religions in India so that in the final outcome the integral Indian approach to the study of religions can be truly dialogical, standing for the relational convergence of Religions in terms of the perspective of pluralistic inclusivism.'[17] One might argue that such jargon very much reflects what has been going on in the research industry of the West, and a truly authentic Indian integral and dialogical approach to the study of religions professed by living people of flesh and blood is yet to be developed. The starting point can be in allowing the fruits of the study of religions and interreligious dialogue to permeate all the disciplines of theological study and ministerial formation. In other words, those who teach biblical subjects, history of Christianity, theology and ethics and pastoral theology and practice need to work out the outlines of their courses in such a way that the students are encouraged to see the connections with the religious beliefs and practices of those people among whom they are going to live and minister. Similarly, teachers of religions need to be capable of relating issues from their subject to those arising from the above branches. And if it is true that the Christian church exists *by* mission and *for* mission, and this is better realised in a minority situation of the church like India, then all these

[16] Quoted, Aleaz, op.cit., 8.

[17] Ibid., 29.

disciplines should be geared to capturing the practical implications in actual ministry. We will have more to say about the dialogical approach later.

So far, we have seen what is happening in Protestant circles. Similar efforts going on in the Roman Catholic circle are worth mentioning. Following the directives of Vatican II, the Catholic Church in India has been more vigorous in the area of the study of other religions and of interreligious dialogue. Study centres, Indian-type monasteries (ashrams) and dialogue commissions in dioceses exemplify this fact. As for the study of religions, Dharmaram College, Bangalore, Satya Nilayam, Chennai (Madras), Jana Deepa Vidyapeeth, Pune and Vidyajyoti, New Delhi have initiated researches, produced scholars and published extensively. Similar discussions with those we have seen above are taking place. Perhaps greater integration of the study of religions with theology and biblical studies has been achieved in Catholic circles. However, the tension between the position maintaining proclamation, witness and the sacramental centre of the Church on the one hand, and the position of truth-seeking continues to remain unresolved. Those who are involved in theological education and priestly training lean towards the latter. For example, the eighth annual meeting of the Indian Theological Association of the Roman Catholic tradition stated:

> A Christian theologian in India today has to be a pilgrim in quest of truth, wherever it may be found. Therefore, a sincere participation in the religious experience of people of other faiths becomes *sine qua non* for our integral grasp and understanding of revelation itself. Hence, in practice, theological education in the context of plurality of religions turns out to be an inter-religious and inter-faith experience of the ultimate which enlightens all peoples revealing itself in various ways and diverse forms. This will be more in the nature of an initiation into a way of life than an academic pursuit.[18]

---

[18] Quoted, Ibid., 12.

This statement matches well with the statements we referred to in connection with the style of theological education in the 'Serampore family.' Perhaps what lies before theological educators in India, both Catholic and Protestant, is to integrate the 'inter-religious experience of the ultimate' and the obligation of Christians to witness to the revelation of that ultimate in and through the Hebrew/Jewish tradition and Jesus Christ.

One common concern in the field of theological education and ministerial formation in India is the production of text books in the vernacular written by Indians. Writing in English of course is a necessity within India as it is the link language between various linguistic regions. But such writing mostly serves to feed into discussions and to fulfil requirements at international level, while members of the regional churches are starving. Another interesting factor is that some of the prominent scholars teaching Religions in theological institutions in India have been non-Indians, and their contribution to production of materials in vernacular is limited. The BTTBPSA (Board for Theological Text Books Programme of South Asia), established in 1982, is aiming to co-ordinate and guide the production of theological text books in the major vernaculars of the region in association with the BTESSC (Board for Theological Education of the Senate of Serampore College). BTTBPSA supports and encourages the vernacular theological text book clubs or committees by giving grants, conducting workshops, producing source materials and sharing news and views through its newsletter, *The Theological Writer*. One of the recent achievements of the BTTBPSA is preparation and publication of guidelines for writing theological text books in India.[19] There is a section in this booklet on 'Perspectives and Procedures' which mentions guidelines in general and then for each branch of study. For 'Religion and Society' they include avoiding bearing false witness against our neighbours of other faiths and ideologies, acknowledging different approaches to the study of religions, giving information about all dimensions of religious life without reducing it to one or two favourite aspects,

[19] See I. Selvanayagam (ed.), *Writing Theological Text Books - Some Guidelines*, Bangalore: BTTBPSA/BTESSC, 1996.

giving adequate illustrations from the primary scriptures or texts, relating themes like creation and salvation to Christian views, and pointing out directions for co-operation and further dialogue. And for 'Mission and Dialogue' the guidelines suggest a spirit of openness, clarity about the true nature of evangelism, the need to mobilise interreligious resources for socio-economic transformation and nation-building, pointing out the danger of interreligious ignorance which is often perpetuated by the slogan of 'one truth and many religions' and by superficial comparison, and emphasising a new approach to our own scripture and tradition as to their relevance in a multi-religious context. The list of books suggested for writing in the above two related areas covers all the major topics. Guidelines for other branches of study include the need to allow interreligious concerns to permeate their text books. The fruits of all such attempts have yet to be seen at both national and regional levels in India.

The British Scene

Compared to India, the British Isles, though tiny as a landscape, present a more varied and complex picture of theological education and ministerial training. On the one hand, the study of religion in its own right has reached the highest places of the academic structure, starting from Religious Education at early levels. On the other hand, however, its influence on the structures of ministerial formation is minimal. This is one of the greatest ironies of a nation with a long-standing Christian tradition and continued pride in its scholarly attraction to the whole world, yet having churches and ministers who are least bothered about what is happening to their next door neighbours of other religions and what they can learn from them. This is in spite of the fact that 'the UK has greater religious diversity than any other country of the European Union.'

The agreed national guidelines of the UK for religious education in schools state that a syllabus must 'reflect the fact that religious traditions of Great Britain are in the main Christian while taking account of other principal religions.' The guidelines suggest that from the age of 5 children should learn about Christianity, and that the five other main religions in Britain (Islam, Hinduism,

Sikhism, Judaism and Buddhism) should be covered by the age of 16. This arrangement represents a stage reached after a long process of consideration and reconsideration of religious education in this country. The source book *Religions in the UK: A Multifaith Directory*, published by the University of Derby in association with the Inter-Faith Network for the United Kingdom, revised every year, provides most useful details. Nevertheless, it has to be said that it has not in any way increased respect for their own religion among the youth, let alone respect for other religions!

Although, the earliest pioneers of comparative religion like Max Müller were based in Britain, the country did not have the honour of establishing the first professorial chair on the subject (which was Switzerland, where teaching started at the University of Basel in 1834 and where a chair was created at Geneva in 1873). Joseph E. Carpenter started to offer courses of lectures in comparative religion in Manchester College based in London in 1876. When the College moved to Oxford in 1889 under his guidance it 'became a notable centre for comparative religious studies'. When Andrew M. Fairbairn became the first principal of the Congregational Mansfield College, Oxford, teaching in comparative religion was introduced in 1886. Eric Sharpe observes:

> Fairbairn's interests, like Carpenter's, were mainly theological; unlike Carpenter, Fairbairn had no major non-Christian field to call his own. But he did exercise a wide influence among generations of Congregational ministers and laymen. He inspired the introduction of courses in comparative religion into the curricula of other theological colleges, not all of them Congregational; and when in 1904 a British University – the University of Manchester – finally established a chair of comparative religion, one of the men mainly responsible was A.S. Peake, who had been a friend and colleague of Fairbairn's at Mansfield College.[20]

Subsequently, comparative religion, history of religion, science of religion or religious studies, as it was variously called,

[20] E.J. Sharpe, *Comparative Religion - A History*, London: Duckworth, 1975, 131.

spread to other universities and occupied an important place. The concerned department's name and structure differs from university to university. For instance, in the University of Derby 'The Religious Studies Subject Area is a part of the Division of Social Science within the University's School of Education and Social Science'. In the case of Cambridge and Birmingham it is part of the Theology Faculty, whereas in Bristol there is a Department of Theology and Religious Studies. Besides this, there are centres for advanced studies of religions like the School of African and Oriental Studies based in London. Fruitful research could be done on how far the study of religions in the universities and such centres in UK is integrated to Christian theology and questions about mission today. Since there is no central body to co-ordinate and monitor consistency, each case needs to be studied separately.

It is a mystery that the original influence of the comparative study of religion could not find expression in the ministerial formation centres of different denominations. Let us consult two examples. Andrew Wingate was trained for the ordained ministry in the Anglican Church in the early 1970s in the then Lincoln Theological College which 'combined openness in theology, a strong liturgical tradition and strong emphasis on the pastoral ministry'. But there was no place for the study of other religions. In the introduction to his remarkable book on theological education in India and UK Wingate writes:

> In the area of world faiths, I trained blissfully ignorant that the majority of the world was not even nominally Christian; Islam never even entered our horizons, and we talked of Judaism only as the religion of Jesus and Paul, not of living Jews as found in large numbers in several of our British cities. Not even the fact that my maternal grandfather was of German Jewish stock brought this home to me. This may have been a consequence of the reality that we thought little of the world church, or of the Anglican Communion beyond the Church of England. Nor did we study, as far

as I remember, the history of the 'mission field' as it was known then, even from a Eurocentric perspective.[21]

'Mission and Evangelism in Methodist Theological Inquiry and Education with special relation to Culture and Context' was the title of a paper that Kenneth Cracknell presented to the World Methodist Conference held at Rio de Janeiro in 1996. The main thrust of this paper was taking mission seriously, with an awareness of challenges of religious and cultural pluralism and the failure of the ministerial formation programmes of the Methodist Church in the past. He points out two strands of what he calls the 'suspicion of theological education in Methodism': glorification of informal training and fierce anti-intellectualism in relation to academic study. Seeking the Holy Spirit's personal inspiration, a combative mentality, respect for elderly ministers as tutors who could impart the pure doctrines, a disciplined life of prayer, cultural superiority, inflexible erudition and enthusiasm in communicating the simple gospel of Jesus Christ were the fundamental characteristics of theological education which continued even after the first formal theological educational institution was established in 1834. 'Many factors militated against the serious study of mission and evangelism, and particularly against investigating the cross-cultural communication and interpretation of the Gospel'. The adventurous spirit of innovation was carefully avoided from the precincts of theological education on the basis that Christianity was the true religion 'given to mankind in a finished form, and is to be learned and not improved'. The inadequacy and inflexibility of the curriculum in Richmond College, for instance, contributed to the failure of the college or Methodism to respond to situations of missionaries encountering other cultures or of a few candidates from overseas who came to this college for training. Comparative Religion somehow got into the system through the special interest and expertise of a few lecturers towards the end of the nineteenth century. According to a testimony, 'lectures on Comparative Religion were the only subjects in the curriculum which had any specific bearing on our work as missionaries.' However, the

[21] A. Wingate, *Theological Education: Does it Make a Difference? – Global Lessons from India and Britain*, Geneva: WCC Publications, 1999, 1.

dominant view of Christianity in relation to other religions among missionaries and trainers was that of 'one truth and many errors'. After pointing out changes in the recent past in attitude, training patterns and the contribution of a host of Methodist scholars to the study of religion, in the concluding part of his paper Cracknell mentions some recent developments which include my appointment to Wesley College, Bristol (1996-2000), and my colleague in TTS Thomas Thangaraj's appointment to the Candler School of Theology in Atlanta (more than two decades from the early 1990s).[22]

At the same time, it should be acknowledged that there were attempts in Britain 'to heighten the awareness of all theological educators that they could no longer go on in the old ways, as though Britain were not a religiously plural land within a religiously plural world'. The first edition of *Theology on Full Alert* (which contained observations, reflections and recommendations of a group of scholars and church leaders), produced in 1984, reflects such attempts. As it is observed in the second and enlarged edition produced after two years (Cracknell & Lamb, 1986), some of the original concerns were taken on board 'by large numbers of theological teachers' although certain institutions in the UK were still sleeping 'the dogmatic slumbers of ages past, and for whom no alarm bells have rung'. And the passionate concerns of the catalyst group, however, could not get adequate programmatic expression in the curricula of the ministerial training institutions.

In 1987 a group of overseas theological educators, under the auspices of the then British Council of Churches, visited a number of establishments of ministerial training in Britain.

In summing up the observation of the visitors, Dr. Brian Russell spoke of how disturbed they had been by our lack of awareness that Britain had now become a multi-cultural and multi-religious society. 'The visitors felt that the British churches were more concerned to keep the old Britain alive rather than address the contemporary situation. Courses on mission, where they existed, envisaged mission

[22] K. Cracknell, "Mission and Evangelism in Methodist Theological Inquiry and Education with special relation to Culture and Context" (Unpublished paper).

as the evangelism of passive objects, rather than mission in the singular as an all-pervasive perspective on Christian gospel and life'.[23]

Since then the situation has been changing, albeit at a slow pace. There are researches being undertaken in the position of ministerial training colleges in Britain with reference to the study of other religions and of interreligious issues. Again, there is no unanimous pattern as these colleges are either denominational or partly ecumenical being affiliated to different validating bodies. Also, there is variation due to the availability of teachers in a particular year. The following examples come from the institutions of my close connection and acquaintance. The Bristol Federation for Theological Education, formed in 1996, could not achieve full sharing of resources and there were a number of impediments, not the least being different affiliations, modules and timetables. Trinity College, an Anglican foundation whose academic programme shared by the Baptist College, was affiliated to the University of Bristol, and Wesley College to the University of the West of England (it has now closed). The word 'religion' used in some of their modules such as 'Science and Religion' and 'Modernity and Religion' means exclusively Christianity. Under the main area called 'Mission, Religion and Communication' the following courses in some measure deal with the World Church and people of other faiths: 'Mission in a Global Context – Concepts and Perspectives', 'Mission in Cross-Cultural Perspective', 'Christian Faith and Current Global Issues', 'Understanding the Muslim World', 'Jewish Thought', 'Trends in World Mission and Ecumenism', 'Christianity and Education in a Plural Society' and 'Christian Presence and Proclamation in Multi-faith Contexts.' Some of these are taught at a different level for MA also. In Wesley College, 'Missiology and World Church Perspectives' was one of the core modules, and the optional modules included Interreligious Studies, Eastern Mysticism and Asian Theology. Besides this, my contribution from world church and inter-faith perspectives was encouraged in relation to other courses related to theology, church history, biblical exegesis and spirituality. One of the MA modules was 'Mission and Ministry in a Pluralist Society.'

---

[23] Tom Stuckey: *Harborne Papers*, No. 32:2.

Moreover, arrangements were made for ministerial candidates to visit worship places in Bristol and to have interaction with members of other religious communities. The 'Interreligious Awareness Week' in Wesley was a unique feature which, apart from new types of prayer and exhibition of interreligious art and literature in the college, brought together scholars and devotees of different religious traditions for various events. And Wesley was an institutional member of the Bristol Inter-faith Group.

The Queen's College Birmingham, (part of the Queen's Foundation, for Ecumenical Theological Education) which is an ecumenical college training ministers together for the Anglican, Methodist and United Reformed Churches, was first affiliated to the local university and, after one or two trials, now contracted for different programmes with Newman Unoversity (local), Durham University and Vrije University Amsterdam. Its earlier module 'Gospel and World Faiths' was changed to 'Inter-faith Studies.' 'Modern Theologians – 3' was structured to focus on religious pluralism. The module on theology and mission was a component of concern about the multi-religious context. As in Wesley, there was an interreligious dialogue interest group in Queen's which organised special programmes and events. A group of Queen's students lived in every year at Handsworth having interaction with the multi-religious community and multi-ethnic churches there and attending seminars. And there are courses and modules on black theology and racism awareness in both Wesley and Queen's. The student exchange that Queen's maintained with TTS since the late eighties added a new dimension to the training in both the colleges, and Wesley also started to do similar programmes. Now the college being part of the Queen's Federation for Ecumenical Theological Education, there have been considerable changes of the curriculum mainly due to change of affiliations or contracts.

Courses offered in the Cambridge Theological Federation (Westcott House, Wesley House, Westminster College, Ridley Hall and some other study centres) for the 'The Certificate of Theology' ('this certificate should be understood as an unusually enhanced one!) include the following titles: 'World Christianity in the Post-War Period', 'Introduction to the Theology of Mission', 'Perspectives on Religious Studies', 'Islam', 'Judaism', and 'Special Subject in the Study of Religions.' In the Northern Federation for Training in Ministry, based in Manchester, for various courses including BA, 'World Faiths' and 'Working with Religious Pluralism' are half-modules each and the other titles include 'Selected Jewish and Christian Texts', 'Learning from the World Church', and 'World Church Study based on Overseas Placement'.

In the subject areas of Church History and Theology offered in the above institutions there may be sections to deal with world church, mission and Christian attitudes to people of other religions, depending on the personal interest of those who write outlines for them. In spite of all these attempts, sadly, none of the above colleges makes a module exclusively on interreligious studies and issues as basic or required. Also, there is no guarantee that the modules mentioned above will be offered every year. The usual excuse is that most of the areas that the students come from and return to are predominantly white, thus not seeing the challenges of religious pluralism for a wider perspective and practice of theology and mission. Lack of experts to teach those modules is another reason as often given.

Unlike in India, theological education and ministerial training is one of the important concerns of the churches in Britain. There are serious discussions taking place about proper modes of training in today's world. For example, *The Making of Ministry – The Report of the Ministerial Training Policy Working Group to the Methodist Council* (1996) was the outcome of a committee discussing the relevant issues for a few years. The 'Principles of Theological Education' mentioned in this report include the assertions that theological education should be 'international, set on a world map and exploring the riches of many cultures and faiths', contextual, ecumenical as well as inter-disciplinary. The report also suggests areas to be covered in a core curriculum. They are sixteen of which the eleventh is 'Mission' which has to take into account paradigms, history, evangelism, social caring, struggle for justice, concern for the integrity of creation, experience and understanding of mission in a particular context (e.g. El Salvador, South Africa, Korea), apologetics, evangelising skills, racial awareness, etc.; the last (!) one is 'Other Religions' which has to deal with history, ecumenical terminology, study of at least one other religious tradition in theory and experience in depth, and ability to understand and work with people from other religious-communities. Discussion on this report has been going on at various levels. At the same time, in the light of this report, from the year 2000 a new pattern of ministerial formation was coming into effect according to which full time residential training in a theological college is *one* of the many options made available for the candidates for ministry. There was anxiety about safeguarding the implementation of the above principles and subject areas wherever and in whatever form the ministerial training takes place. 'A Seamless Robe of Ministerial Training' has been a new feature of the report which envisages ongoing education and training for ministers and suggests ways of achieving it. Whether awareness about the multi-religious milieu with reflection and exposure built into the programme will be kept alive is something for which one has to wait and see.

Towards a Theological and Dialogical Approach

Approach to the study of other religions and to people of other faiths in their living context must be intellectually convincing, emotionally affirming, theologically enlightening and contextually relevant. Otherwise, as we have noticed, students in theological colleges will drift to one of the extremes: fanaticism and indifference. Samartha makes a helpful suggestion when he writes:

> In our pluralistic society we need to overcome the secular indifference to religion which leaves no room for religious values in public life. We also need to overcome the shallow religious tolerance which merely allows religions to co-exist without any creative interaction between them. We need a commitment that requires a sharing of our faith with others. We need a tolerance that makes mutual enrichment possible.[24]

What kind of approach would safeguard this balance? Is the idea of studying religion in its own right of any help? The subject

---

[24] S.J. Samartha, *The Pilgrim Christ*, Bangalore: Asian Trading Corporation, 1994, 118.

area of the study of religion is already loaded with complex methods. Definitions of religion itself require a full course to arrive at minimum clarity. The term 'methodology' is used in various senses by scholars without proper explanation, and it can still be a terrifying term not only for secular students of religions but also for ministerial candidates in theological institutions. The classical approaches – historical, psychological, philosophical, sociological, anthropological, phenomenological, theological and comparative – developed in the western academic world do not always help theological students unless the insights coming from these approaches are carefully interwoven into the Christian theology we wish to develop and the ministry we like to practise. An inter-disciplinary approach can remain an ideal until clear practical guidelines are developed and implemented. A kind of 'genetic modification' in the area of teaching religions, bible, history, ministry and theology needs to emerge. Otherwise the study of religions can end up being loaded with a bundle of information about the world religions while the other subjects remain in their isolated territories.

As we have already noted, 'The Missionary Message' of the Edinburgh WMC 1910 emphasised the 'need for a thorough and sympathetic knowledge of the non-Christian religions by those who labour among them' with an acknowledgement of the 'incalculable harm' done in the past and 'the wholly unnecessary alienation and misunderstanding' created by those 'faithful and devoted men' who were 'imperfectly equipped' to deal with the situation. It further noted that 'adequate training in the home colleges will greatly facilitate the acquisition of that deeper knowledge, in spite of various other types of pressure on a missionary', and that 'provision should be made for thorough teaching in Comparative Religion in all our colleges and training institutions' and 'Lectureships on special religions should also be instituted by endowment and by co-operation, and missionary specialists should be enlisted for this purpose.' The sole purpose of this recommendation, however, is unmistakably to counter the emerging 'spiritual culture' which contributed to the view that Christianity is simply one among the many religions of the world. The 'charity and tolerance' advocated in the report was built on the strength of the conviction 'as to the absoluteness of Christianity':

> One massive conviction animates the whole evidence that Jesus Christ fulfils and supersedes all other religions, and that the day is approaching when to Him every knee shall bow and every tongue confess that he is Lord to the glory of God the Father.[25]

The absoluteness of Christianity and the finality of Jesus Christ was inseparable in the missionary thinking of that time. One might say with reasonable evidence that most of the study of other religions that has been taking place in theological colleges around the world is undergirded by this view. As we have already noted, the academic study of religion in universities hardly takes into consideration the significance of Christian theology and mission. Such mutual isolation may produce two dangerous brands of scholars, i.e., fanatics and agnostics, who are unhelpful for a genuine understanding of religion, theology and mission. However, there has been guidance from some of the finest theological minds towards integration. We would consult one of them.

Paul Tillich was one of the foremost Christian theologians of the twentieth century. His major three-volume work, *Systematic Theology*, continues to draw the serious attention of theologians. Tillich visited Japan in 1960 and had discussion with some Buddhist scholars and leaders. After this visit 'he felt he should start his theological work again, though the third and final volume of his *Systematic Theology* was then in its last phases.' The Brampton Lectures which he delivered in 1961 reflected the change of direction in his thinking. In 1962 he moved from Harvard to Chicago marking a new *hijra* which resulted in the proposal for a marriage of the History of Religion and Christian Theology. He proposed joint seminars in collaboration with Eliade on history of religions and systematic theology which led to a conference on this theme. 'At that conference, on the evening of October 12, 1965, Tillich gave the concluding public lecture entitled, "The Significance of the History

---

[25] *The Missionary Message*, 268.

of Religions for the Systematic Theologian". Early the following morning he suffered a severe heart attack, and ten days later he died. Thus, Tillich's last public words witness to how the encounter with other religions preoccupied him during his last five years.'[26] While this lecture set out most convincing and helpful guidelines for those who think in this area, it must be emphasised that a response of equal merit in terms of 'the significance of Christian theology for the history of religions and vice versa' had yet to be made.

Tillich's premise in this lecture is that religions represent the ultimate concern of human life and that revelation and salvation are available in all genuine religions; so also are human limits of adaptation, as well as distortion. Yet for him there may be 'a central event in the history of religions which unites the positive results of those critical developments in the history of religion in and under which revelatory experiences are going on – an event which, therefore, makes possible a concrete theology that has universalistic significance'. He does not find the history of religions existing alongside the history of culture. 'The sacred does not lie beside the secular, but it is its depths. The sacred is the creative ground and at the same time critical judgement of the secular. But the religious can be this only if it is at the same time a judgement on itself, a judgement which must use the secular as a tool of its own religious self-criticism.' The sacred is both *inside* and *outside* the secular, and therefore God-language is necessary lest secular language absorb the language of religion, which is more enduring in history. Theologians have to break through the two barriers of 'the orthodox-exclusive one and the secular-rejective one'. Any reductionistic tendency needs to be avoided, and this is applicable to the understanding of Jesus also, as he is a divine figure or a social figure. 'Therefore, in order to have a valued, evaluated and significant understanding of the history of religions, one has to break through the Jesus-centred alliance of the opposite poles, the orthodox as well as the secular.' What we need 'is a theology of the history of religions in which the positive valuation of universal revelation balances the critical valuation'. The long and revelatory

[26] Krister Stendahl in his 'Foreword' to Tillich, *Christianity and the Encounter of World Religions*, Minneapolis: Fortress Press, 1994, ix.

history of religions in many ways positively or adversely affected the biblical religion supplied for the understanding of Jesus Christ who appeared at a decisive moment. Further, within the history of the church, the movement of enlightenment and reformation became decisive, and a similar movement can be seen in other religions also, particularly in their sacraments, mystical experiences and ethical-prophetic element. Tillich calls these elements 'the religion of the concrete spirit' which is also the inner *telos.* 'But', he says, 'we cannot identify this religion of the concrete spirit with any actual religion, not even Christianity as a religion.'

However, as a Protestant theologian Tillich believes that the above elements have found the highest expression in Paul's doctrine of the Spirit in which the ecstatic and rational elements, love and knowledge, have become united. In this light he provides a key to understand religions:

> The positive and negative relation of these elements or motives now gives the history of religions its dynamic character. The inner *telos* appears everywhere in the struggle against the demonic resistance of the sacramental basis and the demonic and secularistic distortion of the critics of the sacramental basis. It appears in a fragmentary way in many moments in the history of religions. Therefore, we have to absorb the past history of religions and annihilate in this way; but we have a genuine living tradition that consists in the moments in which this great synthesis became, in a fragmentary way, reality. We can see the whole history of religions in this sense as a fight for the religion of the concrete spirit, a fight of God against religion within religion. And this phrase, a fight of God against religion within religion, could become the key for understanding the otherwise extremely chaotic, or at least seemingly chaotic, history of religions.[27]

The criterion for Christians to recognise the religion of the concrete spirit is the event of the cross. The church has a critical role

[27] Ibid., 72f.

to maintain its own affairs according to the demands of this criterion and to welcome goodness, justice, truth and beauty wherever and in whatever form they are found. And it should be critical of the secular 'quasi-religions' because although they originally appeared liberative, 'they are worse, as we have seen in our century, because they are without the depths and the richness of the genuine religious traditions'.

For Tillich another inner aim of the history of religions is *theonomy*, the law of God, which we have if 'the autonomous forces of knowledge, of aesthetics, of law and morals, point to the ultimate meaning of life'. It appears in the religion of the concrete spirit which is fragmentary with its movement progressive and its fulfilment eschatological. The interpenetration of theology and history of religions, for him, is also a fragmentary manifestation of the theonomy. Further, he advocates 'understanding religious symbols in relation to the social matrix within which they have grown', taking into consideration 'the local surroundings in all their ramifications, both political and economic'. Tillich's last word in this lecture is directed to the theologian:

> His theology remains rooted in its experiential basis. Without this, no theology at all is possible. But he tries to formulate the basic experiences which are universally valid in universally valid statements. The universality of a religious statement does not lie in an all-embracing abstraction which would destroy religion as such but in the depths of every concrete religion. Above all, it lies in the openness to spiritual freedom both from one's own foundation and for one's own foundation.[28]

Admittedly Tillich's own position has the danger of drifting to a kind of 'all-embracing abstraction' and the only way to resist it is to take concrete cases of religious traditions with a special focus on the decisive moments in which 'the religion of the concrete spirit' is clearly evident, as well as the subsequent deviation and distortion. It is the responsibility of the theologians and scholars of religions to

---

[28] Ibid., 78f.

develop clear guidelines for creative reflection and guidance which will be useful for those being trained for ministry.

At the WCC consultation of Kuala Lumpur which we referred to at the beginning of this chapter, there was some discussion about the theological significance of other religions and the relationship between theology and the study of religions. Apart from the repeated call for the recognition of the cosmic presence of Christ as eternal word, some concrete guidelines were suggested. We consult the views of two Indian theological teachers who developed interest in the study of other religions. Thomas Thangaraj, in his paper, after pointing out four models of doing theology in a multifaith context (heresy-orthodoxy model, religion-revelation model, imported-indigenous model and syncretism-particularity model), presents a 'new model for a new consciousness'. Basically, he says,

> What we need is a dialogical theology – a theology shot through and shaped by interfaith dialogue, a theology which is self-consciously dialogical in its content. Here, the question is not so much orthodoxy as orthopraxis.[29]

Then he points out five directions - from fact to imagination, from Christomonism to theocentrism, from singular to plural, from ecclesial community to human community and from communal piety to social justice. His practical suggestions include running inter-disciplinary courses of theology and religions, inclusion of other religions as a theme within theology with exposure and participation in teaching of scholars of other faiths and taking the writings of scholars of other religious traditions on Christianity. He concludes with the following words:

> Christian theology's subject matter is God as revealed in Jesus the Christ. God, who is always in dialogue with God's creation, has made God's dialogue become flesh in Jesus of Nazareth. If this is the vision of God in Christian

---

[29] Thangaraj, "Teaching Theology in a Multi-faith Context: A New Approach to Teaching Systematic Theology" in Amirtham and Ariarajah, Op.cit. 33.

theology, Christian theology cannot afford to be anything but dialogical.[30]

Thangaraj's position and proposal raises number of questions. For instance, how do we understand the nature of the dialogical process represented by the Jewish tradition which gave us a Jesus for the world? How do we account for conflicting truth claims not only between religions, but also between various traditions within a religion like Hinduism? Are there signs for viewing other religious traditions also as representing different dialogical processes? If God's dialogue became flesh in Jesus what is the significance of this event for people of other faiths? What kind of ecclesial community can guarantee faithful commitment to God in Christ at the same time contributing to the development of common human community? Convincing answers to such questions alone can promise a healthy marriage between theology and the study of religions.

Interreligious guest teaching and occasional learning may turn to be teaching one's religion unless strict guidelines and proper ethos are affirmed and followed. There may be other models. Let me cite a promising initiative and miserable failure. While the dialogue programme in TTS was progressing, Thangaraj initiated a Saiva-Christian Study Forum in which about five Saiva scholars and an equal number of Christian scholars studied the key texts of the Bible and the canonical texts of Tamil Saivism together. We met at the house of each member in turn. It proved to be not only novel but also fruitful in terms of developing a close fellowship and promoting Saiva-Christian understanding. Nevertheless, for various reasons including Thangaraj's departure the fellowship could not be sustained.

Samuel Amirtham, then the director of the Programme on Theological Education of the WCC Geneva, initiated a novel programme called MEET (Multifaith Education by Extension in Tamilnadu) in 1984 and made Chellakkan Rajamony (his former student at TTS and presbyter of the Kanyakumari diocese where he worked as the first full time minister of interreligious dialogue under the guidance of bishop Selvamony) as the coordinator. The

[30] Ibid., 35.

main function of this programme was to organise interreligious study groups in which each member would study his or her own scripture and that of others with mutual help by way of explanation and interpretation. Some groups were organised and study materials produced, but the programme has not been fully successful in persuading people to come forward to engage in this study.

Paul Rajashekar in his 'overall assessment' of the Kuala Lumpur consultation points out a 'crossing over' of seeing the world through the eyes of another's tradition which 'enables us to understand ourselves and the particularities of our own tradition in greater depth and clarity'. Further, he states:

> We cannot really know our own – Christian – tradition without knowing at least one other in some depth as well. This capacity to understand the other and to see ourselves through the other's eyes is essential to our understanding of the mission and ministry of the church today and hence for the sake of theologizing. In the context of theological education this means that the study of other religions must be grounded in proper dialogical praxis. Other faiths are to be studied not in an abstract theoretical way but in constant dialogue with the adherents of those faiths.[31]

He also suggests that 'Christians need to cultivate the habit of seeing their religious experience as part of a wider religious experience rather than something apart.' With reference to the Asian hermeneutical context, he suggests that biblical exegesis be done in the light of other scriptures which can be secured by interreligious reading of all scriptures. Again, one can raise a number of questions. For example, what is the purpose of gaining clarity and deeper understanding of our own faith by studying another religion? In what way does it affect our understanding of mission? Is there a common religious experience shared by people of different faiths as claimed by Radhakrishnan when he said that 'all mystics speak the same language?' Moreover, in order to move the 'dialogical praxis' away from a Christian monologue we need the co-operation of those

---

[31] Ibid., 110.

who would also apply the praxis model for understanding their own faith as well as others. What we need are not occasional guests but partners for a sustained dialogue.

From the perspective of the study and teaching of other religions we need to develop a genuine dialogical approach. Understanding religion itself is an ongoing task in this process. As Tillich points out, 'religious symbols are not stones falling from heaven'. The origin and proper location of religious experience is a theological question. The components in the development of a religious tradition such as an ancient vision or experience, established tradition of worship and social life, interaction with other religious traditions, impact of political upheavals, charismatic personalities, myths, institutions and money present a complex picture of a religious tradition. As such, let me suggest, a dialogical approach requires at least five elements.

Firstly, 'commitment and openness' is a fundamental qualification of a Christian student of religion. This has implication for understanding his or her own religious tradition as clearly as possible. As we have indicated, the Judeo-Christian tradition represents a particular dialogical process in which we have clues and particulars for the 'religion of the concrete spirit' or 'the fight of God within religion and against religion'. Jesus provides a norm for us as he symbolises genuine adherence to a religious tradition, both affirming the liberative values and ultimate vision yet criticising deviation and distortion. His cross and resurrection represent a further leap in a dialogical process. However, his 'finality' and the 'absoluteness of Christianity' are not the same. Our adherence to a particular church is valid and even necessary as long as we enjoy the freedom to affirm the distinctive vision and values of our tradition and to criticise any deviation and distortion.

Secondly, it should be admitted that academic study of religion has serious limitation. Basic information is important but yet provisional. Living people are more important than the history of their religious traditions as the 'isms' which are often created quite artificially. Concurrent interaction with and exposure to people of other faiths during the course of a study is very helpful, but it should be realised that they may not be the real representatives. We have sectarians, apologists and even those only nominally religious. The academic study of a particular religion should end with a number of questions for which the answer can be found in the actual living encounter with adherents of that religion in the future.

Thirdly, major world religions should not be studied in mutual isolation but in their inter-connectedness. Let us illustrate with the two main clusters of religious traditions, Semitic and Eastern. Judaism itself has a long process of adaptation and mutation. Jesus Christ and his new movement cannot be separated from Judaism although Christianity represented a bold new step in a long journey and went through another process of adaptation and mutation in relation to the Hellenistic world. Islam, which emerged after five centuries of the birth of Christianity, originated in an environment in which Jewish and Christian presence and possible influence was considerable. There are many stories which point out the cordial relationship that existed between the prophet Mohammed and Jewish and Christian communities. It was not a coincidence that the Qur'an mentions Jews and Christians in a special way as 'people of the book'. A Christian should be excited about the fact that the Jews and Muslims can affirm with them over three-quarters of the Apostles Creed. The difference of course is significant for Christians, but this fact need not devalue the common roots. Also, we Christians need to realise that our self-understanding and communication about the person and work of Jesus the Christ, the unity of God and the relationship between love, freedom and law is by no means much clearer than it was in the time of the Arabian Prophet.

In the case of Eastern traditions, it is reasonable to start with the Vedic religion which was centred in ritual sacrifice which, from a hospitality rite directed to gods and ancestors, developed into a complex mechanism involving the most perplexing structure of priesthood and a belief in the autonomous power of ritual. Although, there is a sacramental dimension securing the 'order' of the universe and society by the orderly performance of the ritual, for various reasons it was countered by a movement outside the Vedic fold. The *Sramana* movement of ancient India, the movement of wandering renouncers, was one of the greatest prophetic movements in Indian history with its emphasis on interiorisation, the egalitarian principle and an anti-caste stand. The Brahmanic reaction to this movement, characterised by suppressing its influence by taking political advantage, incorporating new elements into their system and modifying their own position, was a further step in this process. The amalgamation of the Brahmanic/Vedic tradition with several regional traditions resulted in the more enduring devotional traditions of Vaishnavism and Saivism which, while trying to suppress the influence of Buddhism and Jainism even to the extent of persecuting their adherents, have continued to absorb the diverse popular traditions of India. Further, the 'alien presence' of Islam and Christianity, with their strong missionary appeal and political influence, created a new challenge and tension in the sub-continent. Particularly, the tension between Muslims and Hindus reached a height in such a way that provided an occasion for the emergence of a new religion, i.e., Sikhism, in the seventeenth century, which holds elements coming from Islam and Hinduism. The following centuries saw great movements of reform and renaissance within these religious traditions, particularly Hinduism, although along with them developed a revivalist movement too. Today, while some of the above traditions have gained deep roots outside the continent, and take on new forms, religions in India continue to struggle to understand their nature and role in a secular environment and to modify their position accordingly.

Fourthly, if we have not confused the finality of Christ with the absoluteness of Christianity and have seriously recognised the 'religion of the concrete spirit' in the history of our religious tradition, we can recognise the same in other religions also. It may not always be easy as religious traditions remain so complex. For example, Tillich's key of understanding revelation and salvation may have to be restated with care because of the inbuilt ideas of purity and impurity in the Vedic ritual tradition which have contributed to the creation or perpetuation of caste and untouchability that continue to mar life in India. The key fits more smoothly if we take the renouncers' movement in which one can see more clearly 'the fight of God within religion and against religion'. The further development of this movement in the form of new religious traditions such as Buddhism and Jainism, enables a student of religion to raise more questions about this fascinating dialogical process. In this connection, it should be acknowledged that at least in Asia the contribution of some secular ideologies points out the religion of the concrete spirit and they are significant in effecting changes in religious perceptions, although they have their own tendency to deviate and distort. The failure of these ideologies and the movements therewith to present an enduring and progressive united front in the unsteady political situation of India would speak volumes of this fact. This is not to undervalue their contribution, and theologians like M.M. Thomas had sufficient reason to perceive the work of Christ or Spirit in the Asian revolution in general and the Indian renaissance in particular. P.D. Devanandan, in his study of renascent Hindu traditions and Indian history saw the work of the Spirit in the reform movements of modern India. There are voices able to recover this movement from the enmeshing effect of revivalist movement within 'Hindu India' which often take extreme positions of reaction and violence.

Fifthly, one important feature in the dialogical process of any religious tradition which no student of religion can miss seeing is the change or shift of cohering centres. In Judaism the expected Messiah is supposed to provide such a centre along with the vision of a final judgement. It is a historical fact that a number of charismatic figures, including Jesus, have claimed to be the Messiah. In Islam, apart from the Prophet and a newer vision of God and his judgement, the *Sharia* law is taken to define true submission to the will of God. The shifts of such centres in the Indian religious traditions is much more varied as we encounter a process of polytheistic, henotheistic, monotheistic, monistic, agnostic, theistic and even atheistic positions. In the cultic life of India, enlightened persons like the Buddha or divine-human heroes like Krishna are presented as rallying centres of different strands and values. The Zoroastrian flame and Confucian code of law and virtue may be other examples of such centres. It is in this context a Christian student of other religions would see and present Jesus, as the Christ, Lord, Saviour, eternal Word and cosmic presence, as the unifying and cohering centre. In a theological/dialogical approach these guidelines are fundamental to encouraging the candidate who is a minister in the making to move on raising more relevant questions within a position of commitment and openness.

What is a Minister?

Though this question is raised here at the end of the chapter, it is fundamental to all the above discussion. In spite of all our slogans about the priesthood of all believers and being ministers of whole community, most of our ministers seem to be handling the sacred power in a 'sacramental enclosure'. Home management or domestic chaplaincy gets priority over equipping, coordinating and working alongside the whole people of God to create a catalytic and fascinating presence in the wider community. The way we handle power and authority as serving as a slave as Jesus demonstrated and spontaneously loving people are the prisms of this fascination. This community includes people of other faiths and ideologies also.

In India the central priestly role of the Christian minster is fully secured, not only by holding tightly the handle of word and sacrament, but also taking titles and suffixes that would place them on a par with the priests in Hindu temples. Calling the church buildings with names of Hindu temples and identifying them with Solomon's temple provides an additional safeguard for this erroneous position. Realising the terminological confusion created by the titles of presbyters and bishops the Abel Commission of the Church of South India (1978) suggested the terms *Sangh Sevak* (community servant) for minister and *Pradhana Sevak* (chief servant) for bishop. As it appeared to take away all the prestige and glamour attached to the office of ministers and bishops the suggestion was rejected as radical and impracticable. Enthusiasm about evangelical outreach is seen as requiring no change in the traditional understanding of the church, minister and his/her role, thus being seen as hypocritical and self-defeating. Concern for developing ministers as charismatic personalities with the combination of pastoral and prophetic roles within a corporate ministry in a wider community continues to remain with a group of theologians unwilling to move out from the campuses of theological institutions.

Discussion about the role of a minister was going on in Britain at the end of the millennium. For instance, *The Making of Ministry* report of the Methodist Church defines ministerial roles in Methodism as 'among God's people and in the world; with God and God's people; for God and God's world'. The ministry of the whole people of God is emphasised. The ministers' engagement with 'others' is mentioned as meaning 'individuals, communities and institutions.' Interestingly, despite a radical move on many counts, nowhere are people or communities of other faiths specifically mentioned. Further, the training recommended is aimed to create the minister as a 'reflective practitioner' which is something like being involved in an orthopraxis. Needless to say, that this could be an exciting process if relating to people of other religions is mentioned as one of the important roles of the minister, as was pointed out in one of the discussions we had on this report in Wesley College.

In Kuala Lumpur Rienzie Perera of Sri Lanka in his paper entitled 'Ministerial Formation in a Multi-faith Parish' refers to 'the socio-economic realities which are intrinsically bound to religious realities'. His definition of a multi-religious parish includes 'in addition to the givenness of the particular Christian community, the people who are politically oppressed, economically exploited, culturally despised and socially marginalized, people who happen to be not merely the majority but also the devotees of Buddhism, Hinduism and Islam. It is in dialogue with these people that one needs to evaluate the credibility of the Asian church, the patterns of present ministerial formation and the hope for the future.'[32] Rajashekar writes:

> The orientation of theological education ought to be one which enables students to <u>discover their ministry</u> in an interpenetrative way of living and ministering in the context of the 'parish', and not one of training people for a predetermined ministry. A broadened understanding of pastoral ministry, extending to people of other faiths and no faith, might serve as a necessary corrective to the traditional provincialism in Christian ministry. This implicitly calls for a rethinking of our ecclesiology.[33]

[32] Ibid., 90.

[33] Ibid., 113.

Whether an interreligious church is possible or desirable is a different question. Relating to people of other religions and treating them also as people of God in the broad sense, however, should be desired and initiated by any Christian minister worthy of his/her name and calling. In India, unless there is a deliberate attempt to be shut inside the church, this may happen naturally as ministers in many areas are viewed as community leaders who encounter people of different religions in their day to day life and who are approached for various kinds of help ranging from educational or vocational guidance to counselling in crisis. In the western world, particularly in Britain, ministers need to take special initiative to meet people of other faiths and relate themselves to their communities and organisations. It may look strange in an individualised and insular society, but if ministers are supposed to set a model for creating a counter-culture, the above cannot be an option but a requirement. And theologically and spiritually, only by relating to those who are religiously and culturally different from us can we prove to have a glimpse of the creator of the whole world who is dying to relate to the humans who irrespective of their religious adherence bear God's image, particularly the capacity to love and respond to love.

Chapter 3

Interreligious Prayer-Worship

Can We Pray Together?

Here we have a question that is more controversial than any other in interreligious affairs. The question is taken as the title of *Guidelines on Worship in a Multi-Faith Society* published in 1983 by the Committee for Relations with People of Other Faiths of the then British Council of Churches. It was prepared in continuation of an ongoing discussion on this sensitive topic. For example, as early as 1966 there was a debate on this issue in the Lower House of the Canterbury Convocation. A motion was put down according to which, while interreligious dialogue was welcomed, there was serious concern over the holding of multi-religious services in Christian churches as this would contribute to the perpetuation of the view that all religions are essentially the same. Kenneth Cragg, a bishop and well-known scholar on Islam, 'claimed that there were occasions on which inter-faith worship was appropriate'.

In the next year the General Secretaries of the larger Anglican Missionary Societies and the Secretary of the Missionary and Ecumenical Council of the Church Assembly issued a statement on interreligious services which concluded that 'while true dialogue between Christians and adherents of other religions is to be encouraged, local churches should be strongly advised not to provide for inter-faith services.' Further attempts of the same year made the BCC in 1968 resolve that while the Council affirmed common humanity, dialogue and co-operation with people of other religions and even sympathetic observation of their worship, 'In pursuing these aims, Churches should scrupulously avoid those forms of inter-faith worship which compromise the distinctive faiths of the participants and should ensure that Christian witness is neither distorted nor muted.' It approved 'each religious community doing its worship one after the other in the same place, but not worshipping together in the sense of claiming to share equally in the same act of worship'. Subsequently, a group of clergymen from the Church of England, the free Churches and the Roman Catholic Church, after meeting on some six occasions, produced a document which noted the above discussions, referred to a number of 'interfaith worship events' as appropriate and even necessary, and pointed out the difficulty many sincere Christians felt on this issue, and who could not, with a good conscience, countenance or take part in them.[34]

The Church Pastoral Aid Society published in 1971 a booklet entitled *Can We Pray with the Unconverted?*[35] The booklet used many biblical passages (e.g. Gen. 14:18-21; 20:4,7,17; Ex. 18:12; Num. 22:34ff; 1 Kgs. 17:20-23; Dan. 4:34-37; Jonah 1:14-16) which mention that God heard the prayers of persons outside the fold of the 'people of God' or the prayers of the latter for the wellbeing of the former. It came to the conclusion that 'the Church of England is right to offer its ministry to *all* the people of England, Christian or not, and pray for them and with them.' When avowedly agnostic

---

[34] For details, see M. Braybrook (ed.), *Inter-faith Worship*, London: Galliard, 1974.

[35] E. A. Pratt, *Can we Pray with the Unconverted?*, London: The Church Pastoral Aid Society, 1971.

or atheistic people are allowed to participate in services at rites of passage, some argued, people of other faiths also should be allowed to worship in churches. However, such arguments could not convince those who were suspicious of the matter.

In 1979 a working group of the Archbishops' Consultants on Interfaith Relations produced a report on 'Interfaith Services and Worship.' The report, after recognising the presence of other faith communities in Britain, stated:

> Given this context interfaith services are not contrived or artificial. Indeed, they are likely to increase. However, there are a host of other factors, such as the temptation to stunts, popular syncretism, exploitation by fringe groups, and fascination with the occult, that could all too easily lead to a misuse of interfaith services. These factors may well hinder genuine interfaith relations and dialogue and thus prevent interfaith services being a source of depth and growth. It therefore seems essential that we reflect on the various types of activity involved in interfaith services and offer some distinctions that would stimulate healthy growth rather than the haphazard seeding of a jungle ('Ends and Odds: A Newsletter of and Dialogue Spotlighting the Life and Work of the Church in Interfaith Relations', 1980).[36]

It could distinguish between only three types of service:
A. Christian services with guest participants from other faiths.
B. Interfaith services of the serial multifaith type.
C. Interfaith services with an agreed common order of service.

This classification is inadequate and further clarification is needed as will be made evident later.

Can We Pray Together? was an important document which helped to continue the discussions on the topic taking into consideration what had already gone before and what should be the way forward. The document was produced within the framework of the four principles of dialogue agreed by the BCC which were reaffirmed by its later expanded body, the Council of Churches in

---

[36] No. 22, March 1980: 1.

Britain and Ireland through the same Committee. The present body, Churches Together in Britain and Ireland, has affirmed them. These four principles are:

1. Dialogue begins when people meet each other.
2. Dialogue depends upon mutual understanding and mutual trust.
3. Dialogue makes it possible to share in service to the community.
4. Dialogue becomes the medium of authentic witness.

The document did not fail to refer to the guidelines of a wider body, i.e., the WCC, which had stated:

> Human communities draw together, express, and renew themselves in ritual and worship, and dialogue presumes an attitude of respect for the ritual expressions of the neighbour's community. Dialogue at times includes extending and accepting invitations to visit each other as guests and observers in family and community rituals, ceremonies, and festivals. Such occasions provide excellent opportunities to enhance the mutual understanding of neighbours.
>
> Working together in common projects and activities or visiting in homes and festivals will eventually raise the very difficult and important question of fuller sharing in common prayer, worship or meditation.[37]

These guidelines further acknowledge that 'this is one of the areas of dialogue which is most controversial and most in need of further exploration'. The above document also refers to a statement on the topic made by an earlier document of the BCC, namely, *Relations with People of Other Faiths: Guidelines on Dialogue in Britain* (1981; revised in 1983), which stated that 'rushing into inter-faith worship out of vague feelings of cordiality or denouncing it without examination as apostasy, are alike reprehensible.' Further,

---

[37] *Guidelines on Dialogue*, Geneva: WCC, 1979, part III, paragraph 10.

it is stated in the preface of this document which was produced by the Theological Issues Consultative Group of the above-mentioned Committee:

> It is a subject fraught with heartache as well as filled with challenge, and agreements in this booklet ought not to be seen to hide deep differences of opinion on the subject represented in the Consultative Group and the full Committee alike. On the other hand all of us would want to testify that we have been kept together in our task by the allegiance we hold in common to Christ and his Church **and** by the deep respect we have for our fellow citizens of other faiths. What inconsistencies of approach and concepts still remain in the finished work are due both to the nature of the subject and to the fact that it is genuinely the shared effort of many people.

All such efforts, even with the utmost care and seriousness, however, did not convince those who were suspicious of the whole idea. It was not surprising that 2,000 clergy signed an 'Open Letter to the Leadership of the Church of England' on 6 December 1991 condemning attempts to promote interreligious prayer. If the number of those potential signatories who did not receive the letter and of those who sympathised with but did not sign it were added the figure would be enormous. The following words of one paragraph represent the overall spirit of the letter:

> We desire to love and respect people of other faiths. We acknowledge and respect their rights and freedoms. We wholeheartedly support co-operation in appropriate community, social, moral and political issues between Christians and those of other faiths wherever this is possible. Nevertheless, we believe it to be our Lord's command that his Gospel be clearly proclaimed, openly and sensitively, to all people (including those of other faiths) with the intention that they should come to faith in him for salvation.[38]

[38] *News of Liturgy*, Issue No. 204, December 1991: 1.

The 'Objections to interfaith worship' were claimed to be 'theological, spiritual and, indeed, constitutional', and Article XVIII was quoted for taking the scriptural dictum of salvation by the name of Jesus only. The 'Open Letter' was widely discussed and opinions were varied. It was pointed out that 'inter-faith worship is a vague umbrella phrase and this is the source of much confusion.' Some observed that most of those who signed this were not involved in any inter-faith encounters and their attempt reflected 'not just bad community relations' but 'bad mission'. Others suggested that 'fruitful and Christian discussion of such complex and sensitive questions requires patience, knowledge, honesty and charity.'

Almost as if responding to an explosive situation, the Inter-faith Consultative Group of the Church of England, after careful study and long deliberations undertaken in its Board of Mission, brought out a document of 'questions and suggestions' entitled '*Multi-faith Worship*: Report by the Board of Mission,'[39] with a bold colour printed question mark in the middle. This document tries to point out that the idea is not new as multi-faith services have taken place for decades both in this country and elsewhere and that 'at least some forms of "multi-faith" service are proper, valuable and lawful'. It acknowledges previous documents produced by both churches[40] and, drawing insights from them, it tries to present a more convincing and coherent picture. This and other documents provide guidelines for preparing special orders of service for multi-religious occasions such as weddings, funerals, chaplaincy and school assemblies. Collective worship in schools in Britain has become a serious issue in particular. The 1988 Education Reform Act suggests that collective worship be 'wholly or mainly of a broadly Christian in character'. In a context of many Christian denominations with a state church and of many faiths and cultures, 'speaking to God' is not as easy as 'speaking of God'. Several attempts have been made to simplify the

---

[39] '(GS1011), 12th July, 1992' in General Synod Report of Proceedings, vol. 23, No. 2, 1992.

[40] Apart from those mentioned, the following are most notable: 'Statement on Inter-faith Services', BCC, 1968; P.R. Akehurst and R.W.F. Wootton, *Inter-faith Worship?*, Bramcote Notts: Grove Books, 1977; David Bookless, *Interfaith Worship and Christian Truth*, Bramcote Notts: Grove Worship Series No. 117, 1991.

issue and present a form of prayer acceptable to all.[41] In the light of all these attempts it seems obvious that the British church bodies excel in the Christian world in the area of producing guidelines on dialogue in general and interreligious prayer or worship in particular. The topic has gained such attention that an article on it by a British exponent achieved entry into the most popular dictionary of liturgy and worship.[42] Most of the above materials, will be referred to at the appropriate juncture during the course of this chapter.

The issue of interreligious prayer or worship is a burning one outside of Britain also. For example, in December 1980 the Lutheran Church in America requested the Lutheran Council in the USA, through its Division of Theological Studies, to 'engage in research in the area of inter-faith worship'. A statement was produced as 'Counsel for Lutherans' which, while affirming the value of such worship with mutual consent and theological care and clarity, admits that 'the general counsel for joint interfaith worship must be one of greatest caution.'[43] In 1994, the Office on Inter-Religious Relations of the WCC and the Pontifical Council for Interreligious Dialogue undertook a joint project of reflection on interreligious prayer. The project was carried out in three stages: (a) survey, (b) theological consultation and (c) final meeting, the papers of which were sent for response from three theologians representing the Catholic, Orthodox and Protestant churches. All of them have been published as one volume.[44] There is no claim that the controversy over the issue is settled.

In 1997, The Presbyterian Church of the USA produced a document entitled 'Respectful Presence: An Understanding of Interfaith Prayer and Celebration from a Reformed Christian

---

[41] For a discussion, for instance, see John M. Hull, "Can one speak of God or to God in education?", in *Dare We Speak of God in Public?*, ed. by Frances Young, London: Mowbray, 1995, pp. 22-34.

[42] M. Braybrook, "Inter-faith Worship", *A New Dictionary of Liturgy and Worship*, ed. by J.G. Davies, London: SCM, 1986, 284-286.

[43] For the full statement, see "Interfaith Worship: Counsel for Lutherans", *Current Dialogue*, XII, June 1987, 26-29.

[44] *Interreligious Prayer, Current Dialogue*, Bulletin 98, 1998/2.

Perspective.'[45] The document starts with an acknowledgement of the increasing multi-religious character of the USA and of the more than ten percent of Presbyterians having relationships with people of other religions. It points out instances of people from different religions with common bonds and purpose. It acknowledges that many stand at a distance and observe what is going on, and that there is tension because of awareness of different commitments. There is caution lest we compromise on the revelation of Christ who is still living. Further it is stated:

> Each religious community represented in interfaith prayer and celebration should be recognized as having a distinctive religious tradition. Respectful presence implies that, in spite of the differences this produces, Christians can acknowledge the participants' commitments. Interfaith celebration can therefore potentially transform those who participate in it. Christians can be authentically open to the intimations of the Spirit's presence in the midst of an interfaith gathering and, at the same time, deeply committed to their faith in God through Jesus Christ. They can share with others with integrity, aware that God is present and active in all creation.[46]

The document distinguishes between three occasions: Christians attending other religious worship, vice versa, and praying, worshipping or celebrating together. Welcome, respect, learning and explanation are recommended. 'Interfaith prayer and celebration fit into one of three categories: a focused observance, alternate worship and observation, or worship with mutual commitment.'[47] Planning and preparation will be different for each. In the Appendix, definitions, guidelines, notes and verses from the Bible are given. On the whole, the document does not deal with any of the deeper

---

[45] 'A Document Commended to Congregations and Governing Bodies of the Presbyterian Church (U.S.A.) by the 209th General Assembly (1997) and a Study Guide.' See the document in http://worldinterfaithharmonyweek.com/wp-content/uploads/2010/11/respectfulpresence.pdf.

[46] Paragraph 139.

[47] Paragraph 156.

theological issues involved, particularly with reference to the positions of non-Christian participants in interreligious worship.

In India, some sort of interreligious prayer or worship is not unknown and in fact has been popular in some circles. For instance, in the prayer sessions of Brahmo Samaj, one of the Hindu reform movements of the 19th century, readings and prayers from other traditions were added to cohere around the central point of the Brahman or supreme reality as mentioned in the Upanishads. Gandhi included hymns and readings from different traditions in the evening prayers of his Ashram although, as a staunch Vaishnava Hindu, the last word that came from his lips before he fell to bullets was the name of his favourite deity Ram, one of the descents of Vishnu. The context of encouraging interreligious prayer for him was the communal tension in the country, particularly between Hindus and Muslims. Without engaging in deep theological discussion, he thought interreligious prayer could motivate people to live in peace and harmony. Gandhians everywhere in the country follow this practice without holding any central deity. At times of communal tension and conflict in particular, they and other groups of interreligious dialogue call for common prayer with a view to promoting peace. Such occasions are used by some, especially Hindus, to reinforce the popular slogan through radio and television that all religions are essentially the same. That reveals both the seriousness and superficiality of the matter.

Theological institutions like TTS have attempted to pray together with friends from other faith communities and even to produce interreligious liturgy on special occasions. But most Protestant churches cannot even tolerate their ministers or leaders appearing publicly in a place of worship other than Christian. In the Catholic circle, while the sacramental centrality of the church is tightly held, some ashrams and dialogue centres are vigorous in attempting and promoting interreligious prayers. It is worth mentioning that an influential lay Catholic who lived in the nineteenth century went to the extent of composing interreligious lyrics in Tamil which, without referring to Jesus or any particular figure but within the spirit of outpouring devotion, describe the supremacy of God and the predicament of humanity. His lyrics and other writings meant for Christians seem to point out that 'inter-religious singing (and so worship) can be meaningful and Christian singing more meaningful.'[48] Coming back to the 20th century, a major consultation on 'Sharing Worship' was held in 1988 at the National Biblical Catechetical & Liturgical Centre, Bangalore, a famous Catholic centre of inculturation and interreligious dialogue.[49] The consultation represented the struggle of Catholic theologians in India, with a few guest speakers from Hinduism and Islam, to define and clarify the nature and types of interreligious prayer. While some went to the extreme of affirming the ultimate reality beyond the symbols of the existing religions and the commonality of religious or mystical experience, others exercised greater care in recognising points of both convergence and divergence. At that stage, obviously interreligious prayer or worship was the concern and interest of theologians and experts of interreligious dialogue who had a long way to go to clarify the issue and convince their congregations.

The foregoing survey of events and documents clearly suggests that it is not easy to give a single 'yes' or 'no' to the question 'can we pray together?' The most probable reason is the lack of clarity with regard to such terms as 'prayer' or 'worship' and inadequate recognition of the theological issues involved. We will try to elaborate this with illustrations.

Terminological Clarification

Interreligious prayer or worship needs to be clearly distinguished from some other novel attempts to enrich the practice of prayer or worship, although those attempts may be taken as a moving forward from traditional forms towards the possibility of interreligious prayer. And the subtle yet important difference between prayer and worship also needs to be recognised. The following ten different, yet in some cases overlapping categories, may be helpful.

---

[48] The concluding words of an essay by I. Selvanayagam entitled "Inter-religious Lyrics by a Christian Poet" in *Doing Theology with Poetic Traditions of India*, ed. by J. Patmury, Bangalore: PTCA/SATHRI, 1996, 136-146.

[49] For the papers, prayers and statements see *Sharing in Worship*, ed. by P. Puthanangady, Bangalore: NBCLC, 1988.

1. Interreligious worship is *not* the same as indigenous worship. Christians, particularly in the non-western contexts, often try to incorporate elements from their original cultural and religious traditions such as lyrics, prayers, meditative techniques like yoga, dance and music. It is, however, still Christian worship.

2. Interreligious worship is *not* the same as attending the prayer or worship of another faith community as visitors or guests. We might attend Hindu worship or Muslim prayer or sit with Buddhists for meditation without engaging in interreligious worship. Although we are present there we may not be of the same intent. We might appear to be solemn, reverential and admiring, but that does not mean we are joining them fully. Some of us might use the opportunity to meditate on or pray to God in a Christian way.

3. Interreligious worship is *not* the same as attending a multireligious event of civic or public celebration or a school assembly or observation of a day of Commonwealth or UNO interest. In such events representatives of each religious community will present songs, chants, music and prayers. Some might join in emotionally, some merely admire, others might raise questions and for some it might even appear to be disturbing. The last reaction is natural if a particular group tries in some way to be exhibitionist or apologetic.

4. Interreligious worship is *not quite* the same as when members of different faith communities come together for prayer or observation of silence in the context of a tragedy, communal violence and struggle for justice or for protection of the environment. In such occasions a common human problem or concern overrides all conventional religious observances and theological questions.

5. Interreligious worship is *not quite* the same as an international event of prayer for peace. For example, Pope John Paul II called for a 'world day of prayer for peace' at Assisi in 1986. The response was encouraging, and the event was influential, but 'there was no interreligious prayer as such, since each religious tradition prayed separately.'

6. It is *not clear* whether in world events of interreligious meeting the seeming interreligious prayer or worship is really worthy of its name because of the domination of one religious community in the organisation. For example, at the first World Parliament of

Religions held in Chicago in 1893 'each morning began with silence and the saying together of the Lord's Prayer. The opening and closing sessions included some hymns such as "Lead, Kindly Light".' But we do not know whether there was an interreligious group planning these items. What we do know is that a group of Christians, particularly Unitarians, were in the forefront of the organisation of the whole Parliament.

7. It is *not clear* whether interreligious organisations with a particular theological or philosophical persuasion conducting public prayers on special occasions can be called interreligious prayer in the strict sense of the word. For instance, the Unitarians are noted for their early readiness to include readings and prayers from other traditions in their worship services and for their keen interest in introducing interreligious prayers in public gatherings. Members of organisations like the World Congress of Faiths and the International Association of Religious Freedom share particular affirmations and have no difficulty in organising and participating in interreligious prayers or worship services. 'One of the first large public services in which people of several faiths took part was the memorial service for Sir Francis Younghusband, the founder of the WCF, held at St Martin-in-the-Fields in 1942. On the occasion of the Coronation of Queen Elizabeth II, the WCF arranged a special service of prayer for people of all religions and subsequently for several years arranged an annual All Faiths' service. The Congress of the IARF held in Tokyo in 1984 'had daily devotions, each led by a different tradition in which sometimes a member of another religion was asked to participate. The closing ceremony, in which representatives of all religions took part, included a flower communion and an affirmation of allegiance to the church universal' which, interestingly, 'recognises in all prophets a harmony, in all scriptures a unity, and through all dispensations a continuity.'[50] It is important to acknowledge that there may be people with genuine commitment and openness yet who cannot in their conscience and truthfulness go this far. Again, we do not know whether the above prayers and services were planned jointly by an interreligious group.

---

[50] See M. Braybrook, Op.cit., 284f.

8. We should reiterate that prayers *planned by* Christians who are involved in interreligious dialogue incorporating elements from different religious traditions and using representatives of these traditions, whatever may be the good motive, cannot be called interreligious prayer. I have noticed Roman Catholic organisers of dialogue doing this. Admittedly, I myself have done this. I produced three interreligious liturgies in Tamil incorporating, for example, the Muslim call for worship, Hindu chant of invocation and Christian intercession and readings from the scriptures of these traditions and used them in interreligious meetings at TTS. In fact, I got the consent of other participants, but it was *not prepared jointly*. Hindus were always eager to participate as such events helped them to reinforce their typical position of 'one truth and many religions'; but Muslims hesitated, although friendship overcame their genuine difficulties when they agreed to participate.

9. Distinction has to be made between a single act of prayer and fully-fledged worship. Prayer is either a spontaneous expression of sacred awareness or transcendent dimension, or an outcry at times of crisis, or seeking divine help. To pinpoint, depending on the core of religious visions, one may join the majority of humanity praying to overcome finitude and to seek God's help towards health, wealth, safety and security. Perhaps a minority, by prayer, seeks wisdom and guidance to discern God's will and join in God's solidarity with the victims of injustice and the vulnerable. Further, prayer can be extempore or a form available in the tradition. 'Worship', on the contrary, in Ariarajah's words, 'normally does not refer to a general quest, but to an ordered response to a realised experience of the Sacred within a specific human community. It is significant that the word worship normally does not refer to acts by individuals but of communities. Here, the emphasis is not on "search", "quest" or "exploration" but on "communication", "adoration" and "the confession of the faith" that has drawn a group of persons together, knitting them into a religious community.'[51] At the same time, Muslims use the words prayer and worship interchangeably.

---

[51] W. Ariarajah, in *Current Dialogue*, p. 262f.

10. Whether it is elaborate prayer or worship, if it is interreligious, it *should be planned jointly and carefully* by members of the religious traditions represented in a particular event. They may be generous in sharing different resources for the enrichment of the act of prayer or worship but should be careful about the boundaries of their respective theological and spiritual traditions. They need to do this with confidence and joy, truthfulness and openness, without fear of divine wrath or wrath from their community. If it is an act of like-minded individuals, not of a representative nature, then it is up to them to make it meaningful for their community, yet with sympathy for those who cannot join them. In any case all worship is a human act and therefore it cannot be perfect, and its movement towards perfection depends on the level of meaning it can set and the scope it has for leading people to greater levels of meaning. Thinking of the major traditions, worship may be a ritual act inherited from activity with added devotion by a vision of a deity (Hindu), celebration of liberation and communal bond and response to God's love (Judeo-Christian), a solemn act in obedience to commands with the prescribed postures (Islam) or an outpouring of devotion in remembrance of divine grace with songs and prayers (Sikh). As appropriate, each view has to be shared by the participants.

Silence can have a place in any of the above, but one should not think that silence can cover up the differences or lead to the realisation of a higher truth. For some, true worship starts and ends with silence; for others every word springs from silence and leads to silence as well as vice versa; and still for others if words cannot define the focus and direction of silence, it may not only have contradicting effects but also lead to an abstract and even inauthentic state of mind. Very often silence is suggested as the way forward to pray together without recognising that it can come loaded with theological or metaphysical positions which can try to absorb others' distinctive experiences into their particular, perhaps alien frameworks.

Steps and Slippery Paths

Christians affirm that they believe in one God, creator of heaven, earth and all people. This has implications for a positive approach to prayers and events where the one God is affirmed and approached in a way deemed acceptable. As the 'Counsel for Lutherans' states,

> Our common humanity invites people of different faiths to consider joint worship, for there is a general human condition which is shared among all people which bridges our differences. We all live in that universal state which invites variously felt degrees of a sense of the presence and power of the divinity, of dependency upon each other, and of yearning for harmonious relationship with each other, with nature, and with divinity.[52]

This statement echoes Paul's sermon in the Council of Areopagus at Athens (Acts 17:24-29). Paul did not fail to quote from the poets celebrated by his audience. One may argue that it was merely the preamble on which Paul was going to base his gospel; but the question is whether or not we have taken even this preamble seriously and asked how we can work out its implications for a multi-religious context like ours.

Those who have no opportunity to encounter another form of worship than their own even within the Christian church and have never been exposed to the worship context of the people of other religions may well feel nervous about the issue. But those of us who have had this opportunity think of it as a journey involving moving on, staying out and, if necessary, coming back. My worship life in the beginning was within the context of an ex-Congregationalist church – no altar, no candle and no liturgical art in that simple chapel which was wrongly called 'temple' (*koil* or *alayam*). When I joined TTS, for the first time I was exposed to Anglicans and Lutherans who were familiar with the above symbols and a number of ritual acts. It was not easy for me to understand, appreciate and appropriate them. In addition, the Indian architecture of the seminary chapel, the use of brass lamps, of Tamil forms of musical liturgy and having to sit on the floor of that open chapel together presented a nerve-racking experience. After some years had passed I reached a stage that nowhere else could I feel as at home in worship as in the TTS chapel

[52] "Counsel for Lutherans", 26.

and, I am sure, this has been the experience of most of my fellow-students and colleagues.

There were upsetting moments when I was encountering for the first time at UTC the Orthodox forms of worship which despite its prayers of distilled wisdom and universal outlook appeared to many of us reminiscent of 'black magic', as one student once jokingly remarked. Although I have encountered Orthodox worship elsewhere, I must say, I have still not had enough experience to appreciate the profusion of icons, and complex profusion of ritual acts. More upsetting was when, at the climax of a Catholic mass held in the open air in connection with the inauguration of a Catholic dialogue centre with a focus on friendship in Madurai, the presiding priest announced that non-Catholics were forbidden to receive communion. Immediately I remembered the notice at the entrance of the sanctuary of the major Hindu temple in Madurai that 'non-Hindus are not allowed to go beyond this point'. This was in spite of the fact that I and my Protestant colleagues had had happy moments of working together with Catholic priests on projects like Bible translation at which a word of prayer said by one in the group was a regular event.

Whilst I am open to appreciate different worship patterns, being aware of my Protestant orientation, I do have my own preference. For instance, I have difficulties in accepting rigid forms which do not have room for change; so also chaotic forms with ecstatic demonstrations, created artificially. Worship in spirit and truth requires primarily elements of both familiarity and unpredictability, order and freedom to change, and committed seriousness and joy. For me the most authentic sacred space in the light of what Jesus said and did is the fellowship of people who are gathered with a spiritual bond and common purpose. Any iconic or symbolic presentation that does not help to affirm and promote this is for me problematic.

When I am critical of worship forms within the Christian Church, if I am honest, I cannot have uncritical appreciation for the ways people of other religions worship. When I am in a Hindu temple I admire the outpouring devotion of devotees, but I don't feel inclined to remove my shirt where it is required, to joining a chant addressing different gods and goddesses, to put my hand on the camphor flame which is waved before their idols and to have the red mark or sacred ash on my forehand although I have seen my students and colleagues being quite comfortable with them. Visitors from overseas are excited about these things out of curiosity for the exotic act. While I can appreciate the interpretation that an idol represents 'a transformed embodiment of the divine presence' or 'the gracious condescension of God' making himself dependent on the loving ministration of his devotees, I have difficulty in accepting the way an idol is consecrated involving modified forms of Vedic ritual which is believed to generate power and infuse life into a stone. And also each deity is carrying a long tradition of mythical acts and symbols with which I do not identify myself. Hindus have an extraordinarily generous theology to see different deities as representing different names and forms of one God or reality. They do not hesitate to explain, as done by some priests in Hindu temples in the UK, that the Hindu temple is a supermarket of deities available for personal choice and meeting particular needs. At more grassroots' level practices like blood sacrifice, spirit-possession, rolling on the ground, acts of self-injury by pins, thorn-bearing or hook-swinging and ecstatic dances may be difficult to appreciate not only for Christians but also for moderate Hindus of 'higher' traditions.

The experience in a mosque is different. I admire the commitment of Muslims for daily prayer, five times a day and for submitting to the will of God which is the quintessence of Islam. How it is done, however, raises questions. The manner in which Muslims have to pray is stipulated with minute details in the Qur'an and in the tradition of the Prophet. While I have no difficulty in joining wholeheartedly with some of the prayers addressed to one God, I do have difficulty in appreciating their scrupulousness in setting the direction (to Mecca) and following the lunar time and calendar. As the one who loves freedom in organising worship, while understanding the need to follow strictly a tradition given for the building up of a community and order, I have difficulty in appreciating having to use the same posture and prayer, time after time and day after day. And it is no wonder that exclusion of women from the main area of prayer, with the explanation of possible distraction for men, is not acceptable for many non-Muslims who visit mosques. Of course, there have been changes and adjustments in this regard.

Already it may appear to some that my position is dangerously on the 'slippery path' and to others that I am not adventurous enough. Perhaps, I need to grow in greater maturity, although I have never seen maturity without certain limitations. Someone has said that the test for real appreciation of other faiths is being tempted to do what people of those faiths do. Since I am not tempted to do some of the things I have mentioned above and would even hate to do a few of them, is my appreciation for all the other things not real? While leaving this question for discussion, let me point out the dangerous spots in this path which frighten people, particularly Christians, who refuse to even test the path.

John Hick (1922-2012), a famous philosopher of religion who lived in the Midlands, UK, in his influential book *God and the Universe of Faiths* has proposed a view which he calls 'the Copernican Revolution in the theology of religions'. He asks in the course of his argument:

> May it not be that the different concepts of God, as Yahweh, Allah, Krishna, Param Atma, Holy Trinity, and so on, and likewise the different concepts of the hidden structure of reality, as the eternal emanation of Brahman or as an immense cosmic process culminating in Nirvana, are all images of the divine, each expressing some aspect or range of aspects and yet none by itself fully and exhaustively corresponding to the infinite nature of the ultimate reality?[53]

He further elaborates this question and answers more affirmatively in his later books like *God has Many Names, Three Faiths – One God* and *The Rainbow of Faiths*. A detailed response to this position needs far more space than is available here. There are open critics of Hick. For example, Gavin D'Costa thinks Hick in reality is an exclusivist, as pluralism without clear criteria is untenable. It is interesting to follow the dialogue between the two.

---

[53]J. Hick, *God and the Universe of Faiths*, London: Macmillan, 1975, 140.

We will rather point out some directions for further discussion and see the difficulties in connecting their position with interreligious prayer.

First, for Hick, 'the possibility, indeed the probability, that we have seriously to consider is that many different accounts of the divine reality may be true, though all expressed in imperfect human analogies, but that no one is "the truth, the whole truth, and nothing but the truth".' He refers to the popular Buddhist parable of a group of six blind men touching an elephant and feeling its parts as being like wall, pillar, ploughshare, etc. Questions have been already raised as to the use of this parable for a discussion on religious pluralism. For instance, what is the evidence of the fact that what they sensed is an elephant, and not a tiger? Who saw and can see now the whole elephant? Hick would reply that the parable is only a parable which is designed to make one point and must not be pressed for an analogy of other points. But such questions are valid as he has used this parable for relativising each religion and finding for it some position in the ultimate truth he advocates. Further, members of different faiths may ask about the nature of religious truth, its function and the way it affects peoples' lives. Or does Hick resort to holding an abstract truth as ultimate reality which is higher than all religions, perhaps unwittingly, classing himself among the theosophists of the twentieth century?

Secondly, Hick clarifies his position by claiming that 'the idea we are considering is not that any and every conception of God or of the transcendent is valid, still less all equally valid; but that every conception of the divine which has come out of a great revelatory religious experience and has been tested through a long tradition of worship, and has sustained human faith over centuries of time and in millions of lives, is likely to represent a genuine encounter with the divine reality.' But can he provide criteria to test the validity of particular experiences and traditions which would be acceptable to all Religions? Is longevity and numerical strength a sufficient test? How would he account for the Buddhist and Jaina perceptions invalidating the Hindu positions and such invalidating arguments as takes place between different Hindu traditions? How would he take genuine conversions which make people leave long standing traditions held as valid by millions of people? What should be the proper approach to those who confuse religion with national and cultural identity and pride and who are not made aware of alternative perceptions of ultimate reality?

Thirdly, one would see Hick's understanding of the dynamic traditions of Hinduism as superficial based on his encounter with a few fine Hindus living in the Midlands and California and his siding with modern Hindu apologists. For example, he repeatedly quotes the Rigvedic verse that states that truth is one and the sages name it variously. We have already noted the real context of this verse. The 'truth' here is not undefined and abstract but clearly the all-powerful ritual mechanism of sacrifice which the bird-shaped altar represents. Another favourite verse of Hick comes from the Bhagavad Gita in which Krishna says that 'by whichever way men approach they finally come to him'. Again the historical context is different streams of thought (emphasising action, knowledge or devotion) which appeared to be explosive and which are made to cohere around the new rallying centre of Krishna, the black divine-hero of a shepherd community who had been taken into the brahmanic tradition as their spokesperson.[54] Even within the Hindu traditions many would not see their religion as one way towards Krishna. The Saivas, for instance, would take Lord Siva as their goal, not Krishna who is an avatar of Vishnu. The conscientised Dalits, the worst victims of the caste system in India, would rebel against Krishna as he says that he was the creator of the four castes although he at certain level accepts even the low born Vaisyas, Sudras, and women who approach him in loving devotion (the Dalits are the outcasts). It is ironic that a great philosopher who applies rigorous historical analysis to prove that the Christian idea of 'God incarnate' is a myth and so also the claim for Christian uniqueness, does not do the same in his approach to other religious traditions.

Fourthly, Hick can hardly have any sympathy, or even empathy, for minority Christians living among the majority religious communities around the world. For him, being a Christian is due to

---

[54] For details, see I. Selvanayagam, *Vedic Sacrifice: Challenge and Response*, Delhi: Manohar, 1996, 178-278.

birth in a Christian country and perhaps, as he puts it, he would have been a Hindu if born in India. Indian Christians, on the contrary, have been converts from Hindu traditions and they seem to believe they have sufficient reason not to go back to their original fold in spite of passionate calls and pressures from the revivalist Hindus, some of whom are extremists instigating anti-Christian violence. Indian Christians on the whole live as close neighbours and relatives of Hindus, and the 'Copernican revolution' of Hick is for them an old story as they overwhelmingly hear the slogan of 'one truth and many religions' spoken by a variety of people ranging from philosophers and politicians to illiterate masses.

Fifthly, Hick does not acknowledge the difficulties of committed Christians, or for that matter, members of other religious communities either, when they are asked to think of interreligious worship. Following his suggestion to see the great religious traditions as representing 'encounters from different historical and cultural standpoints with the same infinite divine reality and as such they lead to differently focused awareness of that reality', he states:

> The indications of this are most evident in worship and prayer. What is said about God in the theological treatises of the different faiths is indeed often widely different. But it is in prayer that a belief in God comes alive and does its main work. And when we turn from abstract theology to the living stuff of worship we meet again and again the overlap and confluence of faiths.[55]

Further, he goes on to quote some prayers taken from different religious traditions in support of his position. And he realises the difficulty of talking about prayer addressed to God in the non-theistic traditions within the Buddhist and Hindu thought. Yet he thinks, at least tentatively, that 'it *is* possible that the sense of the divine as non-personal may indeed reflect an aspect of the same infinite reality that is encountered as personal in theistic religious experience.' He resorts to the position of Advaita (non-dualist) Vedanta which makes a distinction between the non-personal Absolute Brahman

---

[55] Hick, Op.cit., 14.

without any quality and the pen-ultimate personal God who has all the supreme qualities. But he does not recognise the fierce arguments of the theistic schools within Vedanta to be convinced of the futility of this distinction. If we take the worship traditions and their theological foundations seriously, we will realise the enormous scale of the difference within, and between themselves and the non-theistic positions.

Moreover, one would raise the most serious question about the 'morality and integrity' of that one reality or God who appears to be responsible for confusing manifestations and commands unless one again takes the theosophist or advaitic position of not applying such limiting moral categories to reality, or the Hindu devotional position of attributing the apparent contradictions to the divine sports of Siva or Vishnu. For example, is it the same reality or God who inspired the Vedic sages to develop a ritual system with a belief in its autonomous power who also inspired Buddha to denounce this system and create an alternative vision and practice? One would have to be extraordinarily generous to take the same Buddha as one of the incarnations of Vishnu as the brahmanic Vaishnava tradition has done. Did the same God or reality who commanded the Jews, Christians and Muslims not to create an image of himself and bow down before it tell the Hindus that he would reside in idols and receive the ministration of the devotees? Is it the same God who gave freedom to Jews and Christians to form their worship in their own way and who gave details of times and postures for Muslims? By raising these questions, I do not suggest that there is no overlap of certain worship traditions, nor do I deny the possibility of divine initiative and human deviation in every religious tradition. My concern is with tendencies to cover up what appear to be irreconcilable differences between religious traditions with the blanket of 'one infinite reality' as the source of all the diversity of religious inspirations and traditions, and then to bind this 'one ultimate reality' with a cord of interfaith prayer or worship.

'Mystery' is another term which is used to cover up these differences and difficulties of understanding. Earlier, we mentioned the difficulty and limitation of this term. People of different faiths in fact do not always define themselves as respondents to a mystery, but believers of what has been revealed without denying the need for growth in understanding and responding fully to it. Braybrook states:

> Ultimate Divine Mystery transcends all our understanding or descriptions. According to Bishop George Appleton, in a sermon to the World Congress of Faiths held in King's College Chapel, London, 1970: 'We stand in worship before the Mystery of the final Reality to whom or to which we give different names, so great and deep and eternal that we can never fully understand or grasp the mystery of His Being.'[56]

One might go on quoting such addresses given on special occasions or prayers of mystics, but what is required in our discussion is to relate the Mystery to the starting point of religious traditions and their visions of fullness or perfection which are relevant to their meaningful lives as limited human beings. For Jews and Christians the name *Yahweh* itself is mysterious and enigmatic, pointing to a being who is ready to bless and liberate the slaves and victims but not to be mastered and domesticated. In the Christian view of growing towards maturity and perfection and moving towards the future the central point of reference is Jesus Christ. In some way this may be true of other religious traditions also. However, with regard to developing a positive attitude towards interfaith worship, those who are committed to a particular vision and tradition may prefer walking on the steps of a clear slope to jumping into slippery paths surrounded by dangerous pits. In the case of many Christians the fear may be real in the face of apparent landslide and torrential slush rushing in the name of different manifestations of one infinite reality or mystery, but even to point out the danger they need to move on to the extent of their ability and, to use a Pauline term, 'the measure of their faith'.

---

[56] Braybrook, in *Dictionary*, 286.

Does the Bible Help?

Interreligious worship in its strict sense is unknown in the Bible. However, there are some insights which might help us to understand the extent to which a Christian can move in this direction. Those who oppose interreligious worship normally point out all the anti-idol passages of the Bible. In a way this is unnecessary because the issue does not arise in relation to the proper practice of interreligious worship. Rather the issue is important in order to be able to appreciate those people of other religions who worship idols, particularly Hindus. It is uncharitable to develop a negative attitude to such worship on the basis of the anti-idol passages as the context there is somewhat different. In most cases in the Bible the material idol is not the issue but the socio-economic-political ideology it can promote, as is clear in the case of Baal worship against which the Israelite prophets were fighting. Such reading can help to develop a proper attitude to idol worship in the Bible, but it does not lead to an acceptance of ministering or bowing down before an idol in worship which is outrightly condemned in the Bible.

Another attempt to take a softer attitude to idol worship is presenting a spiritualised interpretation of idol which is often mentioned in the discussions on interreligious worship. What Bookless writes is typical. He says that:

> Most of the biblical condemnations of idolatry are not of other faiths, but of God's own people. The Jewish sacrificial system became idolatrous when people put their faith in rituals rather than in God. Christians can be guilty of worshipping their traditions, buildings, ministers or even (like the Pharisee in Jesus' parable) making an idol of themselves by exalting their own 'holiness'. In a very real sense, it is possible for anybody, Muslim or Hindu, Jew or Christian, believer or sceptic, to be guilty of idolatry – to worship other gods.[57]

He continues to state that 'it is in a person's attitude of heart that idolatry does or does not occur. We cannot know if something

[57] Brookles, Op.cit., 9.

is idolatrous until we have talked with the worshipper. Orthodox Christians use images, or icons, as "windows into heaven", to help them focus on God. To some Hindus, idols are only aids to worship, not subjects of worship, whereas to others they are believed to possess power in themselves as the particular deity has come to reside in it. We must not forget that the incarnation of Jesus – God as man – is seen as profoundly idolatrous by Judaism and Islam, so the Christian definition of idolatry is somewhat looser than the Jewish.' As said above, such spiritualised interpretations can soften our outright criticism of idol worship, but no way can they minimise the importance of not bowing down to worship an idol or image which is commanded for Jews, Christians and Muslims. Paul's pastoral advice on eating food offered to idols in 1 Cor. 8 (an idol is nothing, and therefore eat boldly if your conscience is clear but be mindful of the weak fellow Christians lest they tend to go back to the worship of idols) does not undermine the seriousness of this command. The helpfulness or danger of worshipping God through an idol is of course a different question for dialogue.

While Christians can defend their position on worshipping God not through an idol, yet 'with courtesy and respect' (1 Pet. 3:15), their openness to different worship patterns of the people of other religions can not only create opportunity to clarify things in friendly dialogue but also, more significantly, to acknowledge certain acts or patterns of their own worship which distort the unique view of Christian worship. We will have more to say about this view when we deal with the distinctiveness of Christian worship. The following references to the Bible might help us develop greater appreciation of other people's worship, incorporate elements from their practices and refine our own patterns of worship.

Abraham once encountered Melchizedek, the king-priest of God Most High, who represented an alien cult prevalent in Canaan. The king-priest blessed Abraham in the name of God Most High, creator of the heavens and the earth. Abraham gave him a tithe of all the booty he had from a victory in battle. In the next moment, when Abraham had to deny the offer from the king of Sodom to take the booty for himself he swore by 'the Lord, God Most High, creator of the heavens and the earth' (Gen. 14:18-22). This principle of appropriating relevant elements perhaps guided the Israelites throughout their history when they encountered other religious traditions as evident in some of their rituals, religious institutions and festivals.

Naaman, a Syrian commander, following the miraculous healing of his leprosy, declared that there was no other god than the Lord of Israel. The excitement of the new convert found expression in his desire to take a load of earth from the Hebrew soil to his place. When this was granted, he shared with Elisha a practical problem: 'In one matter only may the Lord pardon me: when my master goes to the temple of Rimmon to worship, leaning on my arm, and I worship in the temple of Rimmon when he worships there, for this let the Lord pardon me.' The magnanimity and generosity of the great prophet burst out naturally when he 'bade him go in peace' (2 Kings 5:12-19). No sincere Christian can afford to be less pastoral in such a circumstance today.

One verse of the Hebrew Scripture which is often quoted in discussions on interreligious worship is Malachi 1:11: 'From farthest east to farthest west my name is great among the nations, and everywhere incense and pure offerings are presented to my name; for my name is great among the nations, says the Lord of Hosts.' This is a difficult verse to understand as to its context, literary style and content. Hence its giving room for various interpretations.

One might classify the various interpretations of Mal. 1:11 as follows: (a) the early Roman Catholic view that it refers to a prediction of the mass; (b) the view that refers to the Jews of the Diaspora; (c) the syncretistic view that it refers to worship of the high God in all religions; (d) the metaphysical view that understands the prophet to be saying that some pagan worship is better than the present adulterated worship in the temple in Jerusalem; (e) the view of imminent eschatology.[58]

What is to be emphasised is that here there is no suggestion for interreligious worship, but a worship acceptable to God which is

---

[58] R.L. Smith, *World Biblical Commentary, 32: Micah-Malachi*, Waco: Word Books, 1984, 313.

mentioned in the context of admonishing and exhorting his chosen community.

Jesus did not question the status of his community as the one chosen by God for a universal purpose, although he enjoyed the freedom to criticise it with a view to moving it away from all deviation and to fulfilling its mission. His dialogue with the Samaritan woman strikes a rare note about his view of worship. When the woman drew his attention to an ethnic conflict which contributed to a division on the central place of worship – Mount Gerizim or Jerusalem – Jesus, without losing 'courtesy and respect' spoke with confidence the fact of the Jewish line of the story of salvation and the need to move further towards a broader framework of worship. He said:

> Believe me, the time is coming when you will worship the Father neither on this mountain nor in Jerusalem. You Samaritans worship you know not what; we worship what we know. It is from the Jews that salvation comes. But the time is coming, indeed it is already here, when true worshippers will worship the Father in spirit and in truth. These are the worshippers the Father wants. God is spirit, and those who worship him must worship in spirit and truth (Jn. 4:21-24).

What does Jesus mean here? Does he expose a narrow ethnic mentality? Does he advocate a worship which transcends all existing religious traditions? Or does he say something which every worshipper in any religious tradition should take seriously?

Interpretations of this passage are often loaded with theological presuppositions. For example, according to Bultmann, here Jesus 'contrasts the present cultic division with the future, in which every local cult, both Jewish and non-Jewish, will have ceased to be of importance.' For him, 'this is the eschatological age' and 'Jesus' coming is the eschatological 'now', and the truth 'is the reality of God revealed in Jesus, the "Word" of God by which the believers are sanctified'. 'All other worship is untrue.' 'Adequate worship can only be given as an answer to God's miraculous promulgation, and as such is itself miraculous. There can be no true relationship between man and God unless it first be grounded in God's dealing with man. Any attempt by man to establish such a relationship remains within the sphere of human works from which God is unattainable.'[59] While accepting Bultmann's view, Barrett adds that true worship takes place in and through Jesus 'just as he is himself the resurrection' because Jesus himself is the 'truth', 'the faithful fulfilment of God's purposes and thus the anticipation of the future vision of God.'[60] The Pauline interpretation is thus presented with as great vigour as is done by Barth and others. There is no mention of the worship of millions outside the Christian fold and history! There is not even any proper discussion on the difference between Samaritans and Jews who shared the same original vision and tradition and who, for historical reasons, parted ways.

A more recent commentary on the above passage, in fewer words, clarifies this difference:

> Not that Samaritan or Jewish convictions are a matter of indifference. For whereas Samaritan religion accepted the Five Books of Moses and stopped there, Jewish religion added the histories, the prophets, the writings and, under some Greek influence, the Wisdom Books – to which the gospel is closely related. That way lies knowledge of God and of the kind of worshippers he desires.[61]

Grayston underlines the words that 'salvation is from Jews' but for him '*salvation* in the Gospel means the opposite of condemnation, the possibility of coming to the light, of having knowledge of the *truth*, i.e., the real state of things.' It is more reasonable to read the words of Jesus here as meaning that Jews maintained the story of salvation to its fuller length thus preserving a process with both failures and successes and deviations and new initiatives. Grayston seems to capture the special nature of this process when, with reference to the

---

[59] R. Bultmann, *The Gospel of John*, Oxford: Basil Blackwell, 1971, 192.

[60] See C.K. Barrett, *The Gospel According to St John*, Second Edition, London: SPCK, 1978, 237ff.

[61] K. Grayston, *Epworth Commentaries - The Gospel of John*, London: Epworth Press, 1990, 42.

coming time when everywhere people will worship God in spirit and truth, he says that 'This is not a demand that external, cultic worship should be replaced by internal, reflective worship. That contrast was very familiar to Jews and Greeks, but both those forms of worship that belong to the lower world. Jesus indicates a worship that belongs to the upper world, where transforming energy gives access to reality.' One might add other religious or ethnic groups also to the above categories of people. But this cannot minimise the uniqueness and universal significance of the Jewish story of salvation of which the Christian story is an extension. In both the stories perceiving God as Father is important, which may be distinctive from other perceptions. Therefore, it is farfetched to read either interreligious worship or trans-religious worship in the Johannine passage we have consulted. Christians can learn from other religions in cultivating their mind to worship God who is spirit ('invisible and unknowable') in 'spirit and truth'. It is in the sense of an unwavering attention and focused concentration but with full awareness of the story of salvation and the vision of God as the loving Father of all; and this can be an experience attainable in any form and at any place.

When Jesus said that 'you Samaritans worship you know not what; we worship what we know', he meant nothing more than emphasising the above fact of knowing the continued acts of God in the story of salvation. The early apostles seem to have adopted this approach. Cornelius, centurion of an Italian Cohort whom Peter visited after undergoing a 'second conversion', was reported to have been 'a devout man, and he and his whole family joined in *the worship of God*'. Peter affirmed the validity of his worship when he declared that 'God has no favourites, but that in every nation those who are god fearing and do what is right to him are acceptable to him' (Acts 10:2, 34f). Building upon this basis he preached 'the good news of peace through Jesus Christ'. Likewise, Paul in his address in the Council of Areopagus in Athens, after appreciating the uncommon scrupulousness in matters of religion of the Athenians, stated that 'as I was going round looking at the objects of your worship, I noticed among other things an altar bearing the inscription "To an Unknown God". What you worship but do not know – this is what I now proclaim' (17:23). It is not clear whether the 'unknown God' is meant to be one of the many gods worshipped, an undedicated idol or an abstract name for the ultimate reality. In any case, subsequently, as a staunch Jew, he emphasised the creation of one God, the futility of ministering to him in shrines and idols and his closeness to every human being. He quoted from the poets held high by Athenians to this effect. Again, this was a preamble for his declaration of the newly appointed man Jesus as the judge of all. These examples provide insights for Christians to appreciate the religiosity and worship of other people and witness to the gospel of Jesus as a new and decisive factor in the history of salvation. But this is different from worshipping together with people of other faiths irrespective of their vision of God or reality.

Bultmann, in his discussion on the new mode of worship in the 'eschatological age', refers to Rev. 21:22 which states that there will no longer be any temple in the 'new city' which symbolises a new heaven and a new earth. While Bultmann finds that stage as the logical end of the new dispensation under Jesus, Hick proposes a strange logic connecting it with interreligious worship. Following his interpretation of religions (of course one of several interpretations) as representing the cultural and human psychological types responding to the same reality, Hick expresses what may be seen as wishful thinking. He expects the relation between the dominant religious traditions to be 'somewhat like that now obtaining between the different denominations of Christianity in Europe or the United States'. Not only will there be mutual awareness and influence of each other, but also 'with some degree of osmosis of membership through their institutional walls; with a large degree of practical co-operations; and even conceivably with some inter-change of ministry'. If Hick moves away from this narrow Euro-American centricity undergirded with a Christendom consciousness and takes up a World Church perspective where united churches develop faster than in Europe and America with common worship books, for him a new form of united world religion will be imminent.

Let us return to our tracing of biblical insights. Hick finds in John's above vision of the heavenly city an eschatological unity of all religions in which each one is 'both fulfilled and transcended'. Then significant terms lose their capital letter: 'there is no temple

– no christian church or chapel, no jewish synagogue, no hindu or buddhist temple, no muslim mosque, no sikh gurudwara.'[62] As many fundamentalists do, Hick stops with half of a sentence. John's vision continues to state 'for its temple was the sovereign Lord God and the Lamb.' Here is an inclusive vision of all those who worship one God, but with an exclusive addition of a Lamb, 'slain from the foundation of the world', crucified and risen, who continues to remain the rallying centre and goal of the whole of humanity.

On the whole, the Bible provides important insights for approaching the worship and religious life of the people of other religions more positively but praying together or worshipping jointly with them is beyond its scope. To what extent its insights can be stretched to such joint acts depends on one's attitude to and knowledge of the scripture and understanding of worship.

Living in the Atmosphere of Prayer

Whether we like it or not we are surrounded all the time by prayers for us in some way offered by people of different religions. Many of us do not realise it and it is an astonishing fact that we are prayed for by many sincere devotees across religious boundaries. Some realise this when situations arise in particular moments of their life. The following story that comes from the context of South India illustrates such a situation.

A girl in her early twenties travelled from Kanyakumari, the southern-most district of India, to Madurai, the Temple Town of South India, to attend a job interview. She had no previous exposure to life outside her district and she had grown up in an exclusively Christian atmosphere. Her brother saw her off at the departure of her coach and she obviously looked tense as she was travelling in this way for the first time. She was praying in heart and lips for a safe and pleasant journey. To her pleasant surprise, the driver started the coach with an acted prayer of bowing his head down upon the steering wheel and she thanked God that such a devoted man was her driver that day. But after a while she recognised him as a Hindu because his forehead was full of sacred ash and sandal paste with

[62] Hick, Op.cit., 147.

a red mark, and this was shock number one! After three hours of coach journey there was a halt for lunch near a bazaar filled with a number of restaurants. Remembering her brother's advice, she joined other passengers entering a restaurant, but could not proceed because she was upset by the sight of a photo of a Hindu goddess at which food had been offered and incense sticks burning. She came out and tried another one and the experience was the same. To her consolation, she was approached by an elderly man who was sympathetic and understanding as he himself had had a similar experience and invited her to the coach where his wife was waiting with food. They shared the food happily. The girl said, 'I do not know how to thank you; it is indeed God who has brought you both to feed me.' The couple spontaneously replied with stretching their hands upward and raising their eyebrows, 'what does it matter, all praise be to Allah.' The girl realised that they were Muslims, and this was shock number two! She arrived in Madurai with a confused look and was received by a Christian minister. To her third shock the minister who was her family friend hired an auto-rikshaw on the back of which appeared the caption 'Meenakshi is our Guide'! This is the name of the presiding goddess of Madurai. When they reached home, according to the custom, he said a word of prayer thanking God for all those who had helped her in her journey, but she did not say 'Amen'. The further course of the story is that she got the job and a few of her Hindu and Muslim colleagues came to be so friendly that they volunteered to donate blood at a time when this Christian girl had to undergo a surgical operation.

Life in India is full of interreligious experiences. Those who listen to the All India Radio regional services at the start of every morning would not miss the devotional songs and thoughts for the day that come from Hindus, Muslims and Christians. The meat sold by Muslim butchers all over the world carry with it the word *bismillahirrahmanirrahim* which means 'in the name of God, most compassionate and all merciful'. And as I myself have experienced, Christian ministers are approached by members of other religious communities for prayer particularly at times of crisis. At this juncture, one may remember what happened to Paul and his fellow passengers during their troublesome voyage to Rome. Paul encouraged the interreligious travelling community on the board by mentioning his own communication with God as they were heading to a shipwreck. When they got stranded on the island of Malta they encountered a strange kind of people who showed extraordinary kindness and provided hospitality. While Paul did not want to capitalise on the occasion for preaching the gospel, on request he visited the father of the chief magistrate of the island who 'was in bed suffering from recurrent bouts of fever and dysentery' and 'after prayer, laid his hands on him and healed him; whereupon the other sick people on the island came and were cured.' The gratitude in response could not be expressed in words as they could not understand the language of the islanders, but in action, as Luke notes 'They honoured us with many marks of respect, and when we were leaving they put on board the supplies we needed' (Acts 28:8-10). Stories of this sort might abound across religious boundaries.

Such casual experiences of mutual interreligious prayer apart, we need to note that, as studies show, prayer is an essential element of religious life. The famous phenomenological study on prayer from a historical and psychological perspective by Friedrich Heiler is not yet outdated. The following is his summary observation:

> Prayer is the great bond of union of Christendom; and not only of Christendom, but of all (hu)mankind. Prayer is the most tangible proof of the fact that the whole of (hu)mankind is seeking after God; or – to put it more correctly – that it is sought by God. (Hu)mankind at prayer is a proof of the universal *revelation* of God. For it is precisely in prayer that we have revealed to us the *essential* element of all religion...the 'prevenience and givenness' of the grace of God. Prayer is not man's work, or discovery or achievement; but *God's* work in (hu)man(s).[63]

Parrinder's study of *Worship in the World Religions* gives examples of prayer and concern in every religious tradition for the whole world. Whether we like it or not Muslims pray five times a day for the whole of humanity. The Hindu *Gayatri Mantra* which is

[63] F. Heiler, *Prayer*, New York: Oxford University Press, 1932, iv.

recommended for use thrice a day is based on hope for the wellbeing of the whole universe. A *Bodhisattva* (who is an enlightened one) defers his final liberation in order to help the other souls. *Collections* of prayers from across the religious traditions, if read without the knowledge of their source, have appeal to any religious person. However we try, there is no way of purifying our air of interreligious prayers! Nevertheless, one might argue that they do not suggest 'one truth and many religions', nor do they necessarily motivate us for interreligious prayer or worship. The real meaning and content of a prayer gain their highest clarity when it is said consciously with full awareness of one's own distinctive faith framework. At the same time, using too many words with a view to draw public attention (criticised by Jesus), praying for either the conversion or destruction of the 'non-believers', or praying with destructive weapons in our hands cannot but be denounced by sincere and well-meaning persons as fanatical and misguided. The following section tries to present the distinctiveness of Christian worship in the light of discussions on interreligious prayer.

The Distinctiveness of Christian Worship

While not denying 'the many and varied ways' of God's revelation, it is not unreasonable for Christians to evaluate any claim of revelation in the light of God's revelation in his 'Son in this final age' (Heb.1:1f) and to understand their own worship and others' as related to this position. Despite many comparable elements, acts of worship in different religious traditions are as different as are the fundamental theological positions lying behind them. As we have already noted there is incredible variety in forms of worship and religious experiences within the religions. To generalize is misleading. For example, while they are happy with distinctive ways of worship within 'Hinduism', the Hindus give least regard for distinctiveness outside, particularly for the distinctiveness of other religious traditions. This is because of a particular strange theological position which is necessary to keep up a single Hindu identity. But Hindus often upset others by applying the same theology to their differences. Aloysius Pieris rightly observes:

> By accepting all religions as true and equally valid ways of salvation, the Hindu theology of religions (perhaps the oldest such theology in the history of religious thinking) seems paradoxically intolerant of another religion's particularity in the very act of conceding it a place in the Hindu theological household. The Hindu approach tends to neutralise the other religion by absorbing its individuality into the Hindu theological framework.[64]

As we have already mentioned, this attitude finds expression when Hindus are at ease about worshipping in other religious places and with people of other religions. They think it is arrogant and intolerant when they find Christians and Muslims unwilling to worship in Hindu temples. Theirs is a peculiar approach to religious pluralism. In the name of a generous attitude to plurality Hindus often appear to cover up contradictions. This is applied to the socio-economic sphere also, where contradicting factors such secular constitution and religion-based political behaviour, affirmation of the ideal of equality and divisive caste discrimination and untouchability, surplus production and growing economy and poverty, and so on remain in Hindu-dominated India, a great land of striking contrasts. The beautiful image of the rainbow is often wrongly used of Indian life because in reality it is a shattered image with dark spots and cross-lines.

At the same time, the Christian outcry about syncretism and the dilution of Christian uniqueness in interreligious prayer not only represents an overreaction without proper understanding, but does not even lead to taking care about the distinctiveness of Christian worship. Syncretism is mixing elements from different religions to create a single religion; and no one interested in interreligious worship seems to subscribe to such a venture although, as we have already noted, some views and practices might lead to slippery slopes. And those who humbly acknowledge the indebtedness of the Bible to 'alien' ideas and practices will not fear any attempt as long as it leads to what M.M. Thomas calls 'Christ-centred syncretism.'

---

[64] A. Pieris, *Love Meets Wisdom - A Christian Experience of Buddhism*, Maryknoll: Orbis, 1988, 5.

Christ-centredness need not represent an arrogant exclusivism but the central core that in Jesus Christ we see the continued liberation of the Yahweh God (who liberated the Hebrew slaves from Egypt) as he represented and identified with the poor and alienated. Also, he is the inspiration for those who are open to this vision and commit themselves to a life of worship and prayer on the one hand and of solidarity with the victims and vulnerable in society. In this light Christians may evaluate the authentic forms of their spiritual life and its integral relationship to the social life. An awareness of worship in different religious traditions and of discussions on interreligious worship can help Christians launch a new reformation in this area.

The New Testament does not provide rubrics for liturgy, but mentions elements at random like singing praises, praying and supplicating. There is no prescription of time, place and form. The only formula repeated is the eucharistic thanksgiving and prayer said by Jesus (1 Cor. 11:23-25). A few insights, however, can help us to know what is fundamentally distinctive in Christian worship. Liberation and worship are inter-connected as the story of exodus clearly points out. The purpose of the call 'Let my people go' is to worship God in freedom and love. Pharaoh who first refused freedom, at a critical moment asked Moses and people to pray for him but without change of heart; there are many around with such attitude. Worship becomes meaningless if it is not linked to loving God wholeheartedly and loving the neighbour as oneself and to working for the establishment of justice and peace in society. No other religious text emphasises this factor as forcefully as the Hebrew scripture. When Jesus reminded the Pharisees of the text 'I require mercy, not sacrifice', he pointed to a verse of scripture and warned his community against deviation from it (Matt. 9:13; Hos. 6:6). He condemned the magnificent temple building in Jerusalem and foretold its destruction which would be resurrected in the form of his body, 'the body of disciples'. When he said that 'Where two or three meet together in my name, I am there among them' (Matt. 18:20) he taught that sanctity of worship lies in the unity of believers, not in any place or time. His intimate sharing of bread and wine in his last supper with his disciples was later repeated as the central act of worship in the early church. The Pauline guideline for meaningful worship includes mainly self-dedication to a life of living sacrifice and ongoing transformation, singing and praying with spirit and mind and doing everything decently and in order (Rom. 12:1,2; 1 Cor. 14:14,40).

The last book of the Bible presents an open prisoner's experience of worship in spirit and truth and his vision in which corporate worship plays a significant role in the context of a struggle against emperor worship and oppressive structures, thus summarising the distinctive biblical view of worship. Whatever may be the burden of long history and uncritical inculturation that we carry along with our worship traditions, those who want to present the distinctiveness of Christian worship should constantly return to the sacredness of fellowship and the simplicity of worship as evident in the New Testament. It should be in the name of Jesus, meaning to take on ourselves his intent and mission. Also, it is in the name of the Trinity -Father, Son, Holy Spirit-, the supreme vision of a dynamic, moving, mutually sustaining and glorifying, manifesting one at the time or together reality is the ultimate universal model for human unity.

Another term which can describe Christian worship well is

The most distinctive, fascinating and terrifying picture of worship is also found in the last book of the Bible, which we have already noted in passing. The key is the dramatic image of the Lion of Judah turned Lamb with blood marks standing at the centre of the divine throne. Though apparently meek and weak in the face of the wild beasts (the tyrannies of the imperial Rome) it has a different kind of authority and universal presence. The four living creatures (representing the whole of creation) and 24 elders (probably representing 12 Hebrew tribes and 12 apostles) fall down before the Lamb and through songs attribute to him power, wealth, wisdom, strength, honour, glory and praise (Rev. 5). The throne of the Father God, the Lamb as the rallying centre and the energizing Holy Spirit together present a perfect coordination, mutuality and unity that challenge the world's rules and rulers. Here is an unbelievable, stunning and ironical image of being weak in form and powerful in love (just like children and other vulnerable people) projected into the mental image and imagination of Christian worshippers. Unlike others who surrender to the mighty and glamourous, true

Christians who are captured by this vision, surrender their will, ego and strength to a crucified and risen power and witness to the world the transforming power of the gospel.

Another term which can describe Christian worship well is 'celebration', i.e., corporately using all our various gifts to celebrate God's immeasurable grace and beauty which is seen in his creation and revelation. Christians need to guard against any tendency to drift towards begging or manipulating. When Barth says that religion is unbelief and a rebellion against God, primarily he appeals to this tendency which is in his view the opposite of receiving grace with outstretched hands. Even our asking and our praying 'have mercy on me' should be constructed in such a way that they do not undermine this foundation. Sometimes, emotional outpouring in the name of persistence and perseverance in Christian prayer is understood by others as another way of waking up Jesus or God just as in some Hindu shrines in South India devotees burst fire crackers in order to awaken their deity. Even the words like 'approach', 'humble access' and 'invocation' are misleading which may be replaced by thanking for God's waiting, acknowledging how accessible God is and awakening to the presence. Nothing can be a greater irony than if Christians, instead of 'accepting that they are accepted at every moment' and so work vigorously for restoring God's creation, spend their time and energy attempting to win the favour and blessing of God. They have a great opportunity to show to the world that the problem is not with God but with ourselves. This is not to devalue moments of our laughter before God with thanksgiving, our cry for help in suffering, praying for others showing our solidarity with them and our lamentation about injustice just as was the case of the Psalmists.

Listening to the word of God is another important aspect of Christian worship:

> Throughout the core of our tradition the Word of God, in gospel and law, does God's will, is celebrated by those who hear it, and creates and governs their being. Christian worship is the response of Christians to that Word, but it is also the occasion for the Word's proclamation. When

> Christians worship, this Word is proclaimed, heard, and celebrated. Without this Word, that is, when it is kept silent, or when Christian content is absent Christian worship does not take place publicly.[65]

One might add the content of this word in its historical manifestation in human flesh is Jesus Christ. He is the central point of reference in Christian preaching, not only because he revealed to us the will of God for every human being, but also because seeking to do the will of God in prayer was in his every heart.

Seeking the will of God with the pivotal reference to Christ in prayer brings change to the one who prays. As Sadhu Sunder Singh, the most influential Christian in India, a mystic and mendicant, has said, 'When we pray, God is not changed but we are changed into His glorious image and likeness.'[66] This is like, to use some of his analogies, the leaves and flowers of a plant unfolding by the touch of sunlight, eggs being hatched by the heat of the brooding mother bird, and water becoming vapour by the heat of the sun. The direction of this ongoing transformation is towards the perfection and fullness of God and that of his Son who became man in Jesus. Singh sought the will of God in the light of the life of Jesus Christ which resulted into his lifestyle of extreme simplicity, humility and service. Prayer without our action is a superstition and, for example, chains of prayer for Christian unity without consciously engaging in creating it is currently the greatest and universal superstition. It is an insult to the trinitarian God too. We should be clear that God is not the problem to be solved by our fervent prayer but we who glorify God's name with penitence and passionate engagement.

A Provisional Answer to a Problematic Question

This chapter started with a question: Is inter-faith prayer or worship possible or desirable? In the light of the foregoing discussion the answer is manifold: **no** if it is based on the theological/metaphysical

---

[65] "Counsel for Lutherans", 28.

[66] *The Christian Witness of Sadhu Sunder Singh - A Collection of his Writings*, ed. by T. Dayanandan Francis, Madras: CLS, 1989, 91.

presupposition that all or most religions are equally valid ways to God or from God, to the ultimate reality or from the ultimate reality; **no** if it is planned and prepared by one religious group and involving others simply as guests; **yes** if it promotes inter-religious understanding, peace, harmony and co-operation in areas of common concern; **yes** in context of the worship of people of other faiths if a Christian is in good conscience and intent; **yes** if jointly planned and prepared with a clear understanding of both the common ground and the difference and with openness to explore further the implications of this commonality and difference. In this connection serious reflection on interreligious prayer or worship can help Christians (as well as others) to clarify their distinctive position and sharpen the issues so that we approach it with clarity and confidence.

Chapter 4

Interreligious Marriage

Stories

1. According to the United Press of India, Dr. Shantikumar K. Gandhi, great grandson of Mahatma Gandhi, was married to Miss Susan La Force of Struthers, Ohio, on 3-5-69. They were united in a double ceremony, first in the local Methodist Church, followed by a Hindu ceremony conducted by a Brahmin from the Indian Consulate in New York.

   It is difficult to know to what faith the couple owe allegiance. It cannot be both Christian and Hindu; it has to be only one or none. There is however no doubt that they love each other and are pledged to be mutually faithful.

   Marriage is only a social event which entails divine blessing. It is not a religious rite enforced by Churches, temples or mosques for sanctity, however desirable.

Divine grace is not the monopoly of any creed or community. It is universal and all-pervading. 'God is love; and whoever lives in love, lives in God; and God lives in him' (1 John 4:16). If God dwells in those who are filled with love, they are undoubtedly linked and united in life. Divine grace will not be withheld because of caste, colour or creed. 'God treats all people alike. Whoever fears Him and does what is right is acceptable to Him, no matter what race he belongs to' (Acts 10:35).

As Christians we applaud inter-caste marriages among Hindus. When the high caste and low caste are united in matrimony, the Government and the social workers uphold such unions. Inter-caste and mixed marriages promote our hopes and efforts in national integration. We commend it to others, but frown upon it within our own community. We blame couples united by Registrars, but do not deplore our folly in driving them to it. The Roman Catholic Church is more sensible and practical in welcoming mixed marriages to swell its ranks with christened infants. We have not yet perceived the wisdom...

Jesus attended a non-Christian marriage at Cana to bless the couple. This story is repeated in every wedding sermon. And yet, we repel an unbeliever taking a step towards Christ and His followers. Because the step is now through the portals of a Church. We would rather see both man and wife drift away from Church and religion and beget a godless family, than let the believing parties be a blessing to the unbelieving one. Time may heal the breach.

On what authority do we rebel against mixed marriage? None, but the ancient voice of the Reformed Church... Whom God hath joined together let no Church-rule keep asunder.

What the Protestant Church actually demands is that both parties to a wedlock should be *Christians*; and what it can really ensure is only *Church membership*. How can anyone know truly that one is a Christian? Righteousness is not the monopoly of Church members; it is found outside the fold too. Conversely, evil also abounds within and outside the fold. This is evident from the lack of love, understanding and unity all around us within our frigid fellowship.

Non-Christian friends gladly sit through a Christian marriage service in Church to bless the couple. Do we readily respond and take Christ to their days of rejoicing? Worse still, don't we withdraw into our Christian armour when a mixed marriage is in question? Christ can never be convincingly presented to the world by preaching, arguing or censuring. Our religion is Love. The Kingdom of Love can be promoted only by loving action, not by words.

'Let your light shine before men'. Let our practice speak louder than our ancient traditions.[67]

2. In Sri Lanka a Christian girl wanted a church wedding for her and her Hindu boy friend. The minister took the problem to the senior D.T. Niles who said 'According to the existing rules it is impossible.' The minister was visibly disappointed. Niles looked at him and said smiling, 'Do you really believe that God does not bless civil marriages? Some of us are so busy preaching God as our redeemer that we forget that he is the creator!'[68]

3. "Keith and Mary Bagnell both came from loyal Church of England families, and were proud of it...The Bagnells had two children, the eldest of them a delightful and lovely daughter, Elizabeth, who was now studying history at a university some 200 miles away. Keith and Mary were extremely proud of Elizabeth, and since neither had themselves been to university they were appreciative of the opportunities that had come her way...Keith and Mary

[67] C.D. Airan, "Inter-Marriage and Integration", *South India Churchman*, June 1969, 12.

[68] W. Ariarajah, "Dialogue", *South India Churchman*, Feb., 1983, 10.

did worry a little about social life at university. Elizabeth, blonde and blue-eyed with a clear fair skin and a lovely figure, was a girl who attracted attention. That had been obvious in the church youth club, but there they knew the boys who clustered around her. Now they had to trust her to her own judgement of the men who undoubtedly would be attracted to her...The parents could only wait patiently to see if and when she would bring someone home to meet them.

It was not until the end of the final year, just before Keith and Mary were due to go to the graduation ceremony, that Elizabeth brought him home. They had probably expected a pleasant young man from the University Anglican Society. They were introduced to Ananda, and it took them a few attempts to get the name right. Ananda (the name, it was explained, is the Sanskrit word for 'bliss') was in his mid-twenties, slim, with large dark eyes, a shaven head and a small pony tail. When they got over their initial shock, they discovered Ananda to be an engaging young man with a great sense of humour and the ability to talk easily about all sorts of things. Their second surprise was still to come. Elizabeth announced that she and Ananda planned to marry within a few months. Keith and Mary had mixed reactions...What had most surprised them during the course of the first meal they had shared together (after a brief hiatus when Elizabeth had rushed into the kitchen to explain to her mother that she, like Ananda, had become a vegetarian) was the news that Ananda was a practising Buddhist...

The Bagnells were not narrow-minded people, but here was a shock to their cultural and religious assumptions that would take time to assimilate. Their unthinking assumptions that Elizabeth would live the kind of life they had lived, mix with the kind of people they mixed with, and bring her children up in the kind of environment they had known, all seemed to be challenged...

> That evening they were able to begin a series of conversations with Elizabeth and Ananda that helped set their minds at rest. It began with Ananda responding to their questions about what it means to be a Buddhist in Britain, and what it is that Buddhists do in the practice of their religion... (belief in God is not fundamental; the ultimate goal of the transcendental awareness is *nirvana*; meditation in a local Buddhist centre is the regular practice; most important is following the ethical precepts like truthfulness, non-stealing, right sexual conduct and non-violence)...
>
> There seemed to be an attractive simplicity about Buddhism, although it did not appear to be easy to accommodate to an acquisitive and violent world and it clearly made considerable demands upon its adherents. They were not sure how Elizabeth would cope with being married to a Buddhist; would conflicts arise over questions of religious belief and practice? Elizabeth and Ananda had already talked at length about this. The probability was that Elizabeth would retain her Church of England connections. Ananda might go to church with her sometimes. And Elizabeth was interested in attending meditation classes, although she had no intention of becoming a Buddhist. They had some friends who had learned their meditation at a Buddhist centre, but who now regularly attended their local Quaker meeting. That suggested a compromise that might also be attractive to Elizabeth and Ananda. What especially struck Mary and Keith was how much, and how freely, they had spoken in a positive but non-dogmatic way about religion with their prospective son-in-law. And what a nice chap he was! Elizabeth was doing the right thing."[69]

The above three stories are not only fascinating, they are stimulating too for a fruitful discussion on interreligious marriage.

---

[69] P. D. Bishop, *The Christian and People of Other Faiths*, Peterborough: Epworth Press, 1997, 31-35.

The contexts, concerns and viewpoints of the tellers, however, are different. The first story is about a young couple of high socio-economic standing who happened to live in a country which is different from their own. Basing his response on the story the author challenges the Protestant Churches of India which do not encourage and support interreligious marriage. Many enthusiasts of the subject would go along with him. At the same time some, while being sympathetic to his position, would want him to recognise the pastoral issues and some sort of discipline in the church. The second story, probably coming from a rural setting, does not elaborate the above issues, but introduces a theological point made by a famous church leader and theologian. The third story reflects greater understanding, but it does not touch upon the way the marriage was going to be solemnised. Already we have raised issues which go far beyond those the stories themselves tackle. Similar stories abound as evident in the internet and personal knowledge.

Being placed as a religious minority in a traditional society where the influence of the dominant Hindu religious traditions is considerable, the churches in India are in a peculiar situation. At the same time, no one can deny the influence of secular, humanist thinking in modern Indian society; this is often seen in uncritical glorification of any mixed marriage. On the other hand, because parents are not able to cope with new situations affecting the future life of their dear ones, they often end up with the bitter experience of being embarrassed and alienated by their own children when they decide to run away and marry in a Registrar's office. There are frequent popular stories propagated through literature and film of couples discarding publicly their religious symbols and adherence in preference to the odds set before them by their family and society. Thus, adoration of common humanity often turns out to be a mockery of religion and culture. Yet, there is certainly no guarantee that interreligious marriages are more successful than intra-religious marriages. And from a pastoral perspective, while ministers are unwilling to challenge the tradition and rules of their churches in this matter, ironically, many of them take no care to prepare someone who is coming forward to be baptised just for the sake of marrying someone of their own or their parents' choice. There should be the required space between the time of baptism and the wedding for declaring the banns; that is the overriding concern! And there are cases where rushed arrangements prevent arriving at understanding about the religious upbringing of children and subsequent practice of religion, which results in tension in the relationship and even its break-up.

From the viewpoint of mission, a Christian partner can become miserable if he or she is not allowed to practice what s/he believes. And in the name of commonality and tolerance the distinctive faith commitment of one partner may not be respected. This can be frustrating unless that faith is merely nominal. The fact of religious nominalism is something which is not emphasised in discussions on interreligious dialogue. More significantly, in the interest of achieving interreligious marriage the real difference between the religious vision and cultural/doctrinal framework, our traditions are either oversimplified or distorted. This is evident in the media. For instance, in a popular Tamil film (*Samsaram Athu Minsaram*, 1986) a dialogue that tries to overcome the hurdles before a Hindu-Christian marriage identifies Mary with the Hindu goddess Mari. All these problems make the question of interreligious marriage far more serious than its enthusiastic supporters acknowledge.

Studies

The Committee for Relations with People of Other Faiths of the then British Council of Churches brought out a booklet on 'mixed faith marriage' in 1982.[70] This rather brief study aims at presenting the situation and securing pastoral care in such situations. It mentions four brief case-studies of mixed marriage: two between Christians and Muslims, one between Christian and Hindu and the other about a young English couple living together and having a child but without any intention of marriage and the man becoming Muslim by conversion. Each case represents a particular problem, mostly

[70] C. Lamb, *Mixed-Faith Marriage: A Case for Care*, London: BCC, 1982; also available as an appendix in *Love the Stranger - Christian Ministry in Multi-Faith Areas*, by R. Hooker and C. Lamb, London: SPCK, 1986, 143-156.

typical of such marriage or living together. The section on 'Pastoral Task' has the following sub-headings:

> A pastor's main responsibility is to his church members
> Pastors need to have a care for the spiritual integrity of all involved
> Pastors need to be peacemakers
> Pastors must be concerned about the children of the marriage
> Pastors should be alert to practical problems

At the end the booklet points to a few resources and organisations which might help those thinking of interreligious or mixed marriages.

Interfaith Marriage - A Resource by Presbyterian Christians was published in 1989 by the Division of Christian Education of the National Council of Churches of Christ in the USA. It is a document resulting from a team study which 'is intended to assist Christian pastors, chaplains and pastoral counsellors; interfaith couples and their families; and Christian congregations and seminaries in dealing with issues related to interfaith marriages and relationships'. It is produced in the light of the increased number of interreligious marriages in the USA which itself is a complex multi-religious society. According to one source, noted in this document, interreligious marriage in the States 'is up from 6 percent in 1957 to 20 percent in 1990'. The 'Introduction' includes a brief presentation of the sociological and historical context. It is followed by the presentation of the theological frameworks in Christian, Jewish and Islamic traditions. Subsequently a detailed section on 'challenges and opportunities' identifies issues which are first addressed to interreligious couples and their families. They include spiritual growth and well-being of the couple, tendency to strive for the conversion of one spouse to the other's religion, personal problems and inter-personal tensions, occasions of searching for identity, especially in relation to families or country of origin, pre-nuptial agreements and legal issues, the birth of children, family worship and celebration of life-cycle, and challenges in time management and in maintaining relationships to the communities of each spouse. The only point of opportunity suggested is being a bridge between two faith communities. The picture, however, looks rather idealist and the exhortation is demanding:

> The interfaith couple or family might be a ***bridge between two faith communities***, a witness to the majesty and mystery of God's ways with humankind, as they become visible in the wider community. The couple may be challenged to accept their role as bridge-builders of a world community in which justice, morality, kindness, and peace will prevail.
>
> Building bridges from oneself to another requires a mature self-awareness. Awareness of one's own values and beliefs and sensitivity to those of the spouse implies a readiness to appreciate, discuss and grow in response to the events, behaviours, and circumstances that shape the shared life of marriage. A willingness to explore the traditions, beliefs, history, and community of the spouse's faith can bring understanding as well as shared growth that is corporately owned by the couple. In such an invested interfaith dialogue, individuals often become true bridge-builders between faith communities, as they stimulate a deep level of reflection and help to raise the surrounding community to a higher consciousness of understanding, as they quietly, and usually unconsciously, overcome barriers of hostility between faith communities.[71]

Following a description of each of the above issues and opportunity, a probing question is given to the couple about their commitment to faith as well as to marriage. Similarly, there are responsibilities put forward to the community or congregation. They include:

> 1. Special attempts may be made to ***support and include the couple in the ongoing life and activities of the church...***

[71] Ibid., 23.

2. ***The support and inclusion of the children*** of interfaith marriages are equally valuable to the family and congregation...
3. The ***education of the congregation in the understanding of another faith*** is a unique opportunity...
4. ***The pastor and other church leadership should be theologically aware and trained for this new venture...***
5. ***The wider community should be involved*** as well in making a positive affirmation of the interfaith couple and of the other community represented in the marriage...

Again, each statement and its elaboration is followed by a question addressed to the pastor.

Further, the document recounts eleven stories of interreligious marriage, all between Jews, Christians and Muslims. These stories seem to challenge the ideal vision stated above as they point out a number of problems in the actual life of the interreligious couple, compounded and complicated by the expectations of in-laws and of traditions. Appropriately, one of the conclusions of the document is the following:

> Each couple is unique and there is no one rule applicable to all. An extensive premarital counselling process, and any marital counselling, should raise to the couple's consciousness those values, issues, questions, expectations, and assumptions they bring to the marriage. As with all marriages, not all questions can be answered before the fact. The couple must commit themselves to the common struggle. While all marriages require negotiation and compromise, those skills are all the more necessary in an interfaith marriage. They go with the territory. Together with the sometimes daunting challenges, interfaith marriage can also provide an opportunity for tremendous growth in self-awareness and in companionship.[72]

---

[72] Ibid., 33f.

Thus far we have covered only part I of this important document. Part II starts with a section on 'questions for counsellors, couples, and groups'. The next section provides 'sample liturgical resources' from a Christian-Muslim wedding, a Christian-Jewish wedding (two liturgies) and the following section gives two sample marriage contracts, one Jewish and the other Muslim. The final section provides a useful annotated bibliography and contact addresses for further advice.

More recently, on behalf of the Islam in Europe Committee of the Conference of European Churches and Council of European Episcopal Conferences, CCBI brought out a booklet on Christian-Muslim marriage.[73] German, French and Italian versions of this booklet are also available and translations into other European languages such as Norwegian and Dutch were being considered. The booklet starts with a presentation of the situation in Europe where Christian-Muslim marriage is a significant issue. It moves on to a detailed discussion on Christian understanding of marriage with reference to the scope and theological position of various Churches. Further, family and marriage in Islam is discussed with reference to Qur'anic injunctions, schools of Islamic law and distinctive positions in different Muslim countries. The ministerial task which is the special concern of the guidelines is then taken, with emphasis on ongoing concerns, the responsibility of the churches, a frame of reference, five phases (the contact phase, the phase of decision making, the preparatory phase, the phase for pastoral care and the phase of the end of marriage) in counselling and pastoral care, marriage contract to prevent problems and suggestions for a good attitude on the part of the minister. The final section on special pastoral concerns elaborates those five phases giving helpful information on the various positions of a church wedding. A bibliography and useful contact addresses are given at the end.

The WCC's OIRR (Office on Inter-Religious Relations) and the Vatican's PCID (Pontifical Council for Inter-religious Dialogue) launched a project in 1994 and the result was 'Reflections on

[73] C. Lamb (ed.), *Marriages between Christians and Muslims - Pastoral Guidelines for Christians and Churches in Europe*, London: CCBI, 1998.

Interreligious Marriage: A joint study document.'[74] The reflections, however, are very general, and are 'of a pastoral nature'. It is emphasised that the document is 'not a doctrinal statement, not a study of marriage according to the different religions, not a recommendation for interreligious marriage'. The project was launched 'by way of an enquiry'. 'Questionnaires were prepared and sent out to different churches and communities. The answers to these questionnaires form the basis of the first part [of the document]. The second part takes stock of some of the material already produced by churches and Christian communities on this matter. The third part presents, in a brief but more systematic fashion, some reflections on aspects of interreligious marriages thrown into light by the enquiry and the resource material.' Christian and non-Christian spouses expressed the difficulty of maintaining their religious commitment, and their real position differed from individual to individual. The right to religious freedom, tendency to use religious difference as a weapon to belabour the partner in conflict situations, the possibility of enriching interreligious understanding by maintaining consciously the religious differences, mutual agreement on bringing up children, the question of religious education in schools and the relations with the Christian community are the issues identified for consideration with helpful notes to initiate a discussion.

The bibliography given in the above documents shows what is discussed and produced in different parts around the world, mainly Europe and America. For example, The Board of Mission Inter-Faith Consultative Group of the Church of England brought out in 1992 a 12-page guidelines for the clergy for the celebration of interreligious marriages in Church. In many of these studies inter-racial, inter-cultural and inter-national marriages are mixed with interreligious marriage. However, we will limit the scope to include only issues arising from those marriages studied in which religion and adherence to a particular religious community are primary concerns.

---

[74] See *Pro Dialogo*, No. 96 (1997/3), Vatican City, 324-339.

Scriptural Insights

The Hebrew scripture connects marriage in a marvellous way to God's creative will and universal plan. Marriage was part of the natural and original blessing from the time of creation. According to the first creation story of Genesis:

> God created human beings in his own image; in the image of God he created them; male and female he created them. God blessed them and said to them, 'Be fruitful and increase, fill the earth' (Gen.1:27f).

In connection with a discussion on divorce, Jesus referred to this passage and declared 'What therefore God has joined together, let no man put asunder' (Mt. 19:4-6; Mk. 10:6-9). The second story of creation is more dramatic. God was concerned to create a partner suited to man, and an element of mystery is attached to the creation of the partner of the opposite sex. 'The Lord God then put the man into a deep sleep and, while he slept, he took one of the man's ribs and closed up the flesh over the place' (Gen.2:21). God not only built up that rib into a woman, but also chose to walk with her just like a father of a bride when he brought her to the man. The man's first spoken word recorded in the scripture or, 'the first cry of love heard on earth', is:

> This one at last is bone from my bones, flesh from my flesh!
>
> She shall be called woman, for from man was she taken (v. 23).

The mutual companionship, complementarity and perfection between a man and woman was thus sealed as a holy institution for the continuation of human race. There is no other explanation than this inherent attraction for the opposite sex in every human being and falling in love with someone with a desire to build up a relationship of profound communion for which he or she or both are willing to transcend their religious boundaries. Scripture is not shy of this relationship and it uses the analogy of the relationship between bridegroom and bride or husband and wife for describing the relationship between God and his chosen people in the Hebrew scripture (e.g. Is. 54:4ff; 62:4ff; Jer. 2:2; Ez. 16:7ff; Hos. 2:19) and between Christ and his Church in the New Testament (e.g. 2 Cor. 11:2; Eph. 5:22ff; Rev. 19:7ff; 22:7). Jesus enjoyed attending with his disciples and mother a wedding at Cana, where he changed water into wine, thus solving a crisis, relieving the marriage party of embarrassment and manifesting his glory (Jn. 2:1ff). He used symbolic pictures of a wedding ceremony and a wedding feast, to describe the messianic era or the new age of God's reign (Mt. 25:1-13; Mk. 2:19ff; Lk. 12:36ff; Jn. 3:29ff). All these indicate, however, the sanctity attached to marriage in general, but can they as such support interreligious marriage?

Interreligious marriage as it is understood today was unknown in scripture. At the same time, there are hints that enable us to approach the issue with an open mind. One can straight away say that famous biblical figures like Abraham and David took wives from outside, although at one level they were zealous in safeguarding their own distinctive communal identity. The latter attitude shows not so much awareness of ethnic identity as of a special relationship with God and his chosen community between whom there was a covenant. It might look like a concern for racial purity and a sense of superiority, but as far as the original vision was concerned it was to build up a model community according to God's law which would attract the nations around. No other writer was more concerned about the special purpose of God's people for the whole of humanity in this way than the writer of Deuteronomy:

> I have taught you statutes and laws, as the Lord my God commanded me; see that you keep them when you go into and occupy the land. Observe them carefully, for thereby you will display your wisdom and understanding to other peoples. When they hear about all these statutes, they will say, 'What a wise and understanding people this great nation is!' What great nation has a god close at hand as the Lord our God is close to us whenever we call to him? What great nation is there whose statutes and laws are so just, as

> is all this code of laws which I am setting before you today? (Deut. 4:5-8).

This vision was reaffirmed by the prophets when they understood their community as a light to the nations. Nations will look to this community for guidance in matters of justice and peace. They envisaged a day on which a scion from the root of Jesse would be seen, marking a new era characterised by justice and peace, when he 'will arise like a standard to rally the peoples; the nations will resort to him, and his abode will be glorious' (Is. 11:10). But there were forces to blur this vision in the context of interaction with outsiders. This is evident in the stories of how the Israelites dealt with foreign wives. We will illustrate this by taking a chain of events.

The Deuteronomic injunction with regard to foreign wives when they would enter the promised land is this:

> You must not intermarry with them, giving your daughters to their sons or taking their daughters for your sons, because if you do, they will draw your children away from the Lord to serve other gods. Then the anger of the Lord will be roused against you and he will soon destroy you (Deut. 7:3,4).

While the Israelites themselves were a mixture of many ethnic groups and they adapted many customs and laws from their neighbouring peoples, why was such a harsh warning given? If we take the scholarly view that the book of Deuteronomy was produced in the post-Solomon era in connection with King Josiah's reform in the seventh century, the answer is simple and clear. Solomon, wise turned wicked, wreaked havoc in the history of Israel as was evident in his autocratic political behaviour and oppressive economic system. It was mainly connected with his compromising foreign policy and excessive erotic behaviour. As it is recorded,

> King Solomon loved many foreign women; in addition to Pharaoh's daughter...from the nations with whom the Lord had forbidden the Israelites to intermarry...But Solomon was devoted to them and loved them dearly...and they

> influenced him, for as he grew old, his wives turned his heart to follow other gods, and he did not remain wholly loyal to the Lord his God...Thus, Solomon did what was wrong in the eyes of the Lord...He built a shrine for Kemosh, the loathsome god of Moab...These things he did for the gods to whom all his foreign wives burnt offerings and made sacrifices.
>
> The Lord was angry with Solomon because his heart had turned away from the Lord the God of Israel, who had appeared to him twice, and had strictly commanded him not to follow other gods...(1 Kings 11:1-10).

Turning away from the Lord God and following other gods was not simply a religious apostasy for Israelites; more significantly, it was adopting a socio-economic-political policy which was contrary to the ideals of justice, love and peace which were considered to be corner-stones of a model community. The terrible tension and conflict it created could be clearly seen in the policy of King Ahab and his foreign wife Jezebel with whom the prophet Elijah was in conflict. The whole Hebrew prophetic movement in a way was involved in such a conflict for which the root cause was the influence of foreign wives.

Extra care should not hamper creative ways of relating to people of other religions! This was the case when those in exile in Babylon refused to mingle with the natives, and their stubbornness is succinctly described in Ps. 137.

They appeared to miss a decisive moment for seeing their Lord as the God of all nations. At this juncture, Jeremiah, who was aware of the past history and the part in it of the Deuteronomic reform of King Josiah, wrote an interesting letter on behalf of the God of Israel to all the exiles in Babylon. The following is an extract from this letter:

> Build houses and live in them; plant gardens and eat the produce; marry wives and rear families; choose wives for your sons and give your daughters to husbands, so that they may bear sons and daughters. Increase there and do

> not dwindle away. Seek the welfare of any city to which I have exiled you, and pray to the Lord for it; on its welfare your welfare will depend (Jer. 29:5-7).

Although intermarrying is not specifically mentioned in this letter, there is every reason to believe that some men by implication thought so. Consequently, when the community returned to Jerusalem around 539 BCE their foreign wives accompanied them. They created a problem for Ezra and Nehemiah who were busily involved in rebuilding the community and renewing the covenant relationship. We read of officials approaching Ezra and saying:

> The people of Israel, including even priests and Levites, have not kept themselves apart from the alien population and from the abominable practices of the Canaanites, Hittites, Perizzites, Jebusites, Ammonites, Moabites, Egyptians, and Amorites. They have taken women of these nations as wives for themselves and their sons, so that the holy race has become mixed with the alien population; and leaders and magistrates have been the chief offenders (Ez. 9:1,2).

The most upsetting fact for the community builders was that 'Half their children spoke the language of Ashdod or of one of the other peoples but could not speak the language of the Jews' (Neh. 13:24). Ezra tore his robe and mantle; he plucked tufts from his beard and hair of his head and sat appalled (Ez. 9:3). He prayed and made confession and prostrated himself in tears before the house of God. There gathered round him a vast throng of Israelites, men, women, and children, and there was widespread lamentation among the crowd (10:1,2). One family head came forward confessing on behalf of all offenders that they had broken faith with God in taking foreign wives and pledging themselves to get rid of all such wives with their children. But Ezra was still mourning for the unfaithfulness of the returned exiles. Nehemiah did not fail to remember the atrocious and wicked life of Solomon because of his foreign women (Neh. 13:26) 'A proclamation was issued throughout Judah and Jerusalem directing all the returned exiles to assemble at Jerusalem. If any failed to arrive within three days, as decided by the chief officers and elders, they were to have all their property confiscated and would themselves be excluded from the community that had come from exile' (10:7,8). Accordingly, they assembled and made a pledge to dismiss all foreign wives and their children; some asked for enough time to do so and a few opposed the whole idea. The book of Ezra ends with a list of family heads who obeyed the order and a concluding note that 'All these had married foreign women, and they dismissed them, together with their children' (10:44).

According to Nehemiah, he argued with the offenders and reviled them, beat some of them and tore out their hair and made them pledge to get rid of their foreign wives. Thus he claims that he purified the community from everything foreign (Neh. 13:25-30).

However critical may have been the historical situation causing such a cruel act of getting rid of foreign wives, was this the only solution? Ezra and Nehemiah did not elaborate in their books the case of those who opposed the whole drama. It stands to reason that the author of the book of Ruth was sympathetic to them if not one among them. He records the story of a Moabite daughter-in-law who became a widow. Ruth, despite discouraging words from her mother-in law Naomi, persisted in following her when she returned to her homeland Judah, to the village of Bethlehem. Ruth's words reflect a reasoned statement:

> Do not urge me to go back and desert you. Where you go, I shall go, and where you stay, I shall stay. Your people will be my people, and your God my God. Where you die, I shall die, and there be buried. I solemnly declare before the Lord that nothing but death will part me from you (Ruth 1:16,17).

The author seems to propose this as a solution to the dilemma before Ezra and Nehemiah. That means, those who accepted the community and God of the Israelites should not be sent away. The tradition he quotes is linked with David and thus the boy given birth by Ruth, a foreign woman, was his grandfather. The story in any case is not of an interreligious marriage but of a solution in a critical moment when being expected to get rid of those dear ones who had lived for a considerable time and borne children for the Israelite men.

In the New Testament there is no mention of interreligious marriage although Matthew in his genealogy mentions Ruth and three other foreign wives (Tamar, Rahab, and the 'wife of Uriah'). Interestingly these were the only women mentioned in the genealogy (Mt. 1:1-16). It is in this light of a generous approach to the new converts from of the Gentiles (Acts 15) we should read Paul's warning against 'a believer joining with an unbeliever.' In the following note he asks, 'Can there be a compact between the temple of God and idols?' (2 Cor. 6:15f). It is not directly about interreligious marriage but about any relationship of the believer with certain Gentile customs. The mention of darkness, wickedness, Belial (presumably a figure in devil worship), and idol together suggest a low form of cult which involved indecent practices including fornication. It was warning for a new convert placed in a precarious situation which might lead him/her to revert to old practices. There was a group of so-called Christians who led an immoral life, or was extortionate, idolatrous, slanderers, drunkards and swindlers (1 Cor. 5:11).

In another context, Paul was confronted with marriages in which only one spouse had become a Christian. Paul's own opinion strikes a profound chord:

> If a Christian has a wife who is not a believer, and she is willing to live with him, he must not divorce her; and if a woman has a husband who is not believer, and he is willing to live with her, she must not divorce him. For the husband now belongs to God through his Christian wife, and the wife through her Christian husband. Otherwise your children would not belong to God, whereas in fact they do. If however the unbelieving partner wishes for a separation, it should be granted; in such cases the Christian husband or wife is not bound by the marriage. God's call is a call to live in peace. But remember: a wife may save her husband; and a husband may save his wife (1 Cor. 7:12-16).

As we will see later, some Churches allow interreligious marriage on the precise foundation laid by Paul. If mutual saving and sanctifying is possible in a marital union, a Christian not only may tolerate such union but also aspire for it if he or she is truly committed.

Sense, Sensation and Sensitivity

Marital union in general is a delicate one, and it can either become as thin as an egg-shell or as strong as an iron-pillar. Two persons of opposite sex and of different origin and background can make life exciting if everything goes on well, or miserable if there is permanent misunderstanding and disliking. The form of marriage and the pressure from the wider family and society can contribute either way. Those who perceive the meaning of their own life only in relation to the wider family, society and religion cannot get away from such pressure. And those who claim to be free of such dependency do not seem to provide a healthy alternative either. Further, no form of marriage seems to be perfect. Although, the arranged marriage has the advantage of having collective consideration, careful choice and commitment of parents and relatives for continued support, it can drift into a kind of forced condition, from which many do not find the means to escape. Personal choice and long acquaintance allows thorough and mutual personal consideration, but there is no guarantee that it is more enjoyable and enduring. In both types it requires profound determination in love, patient waiting to know more of the other and mutual openness to grow in love, understanding and purpose. The worst victims of a broken marriage are the children, who are often confused lacking stability as they are forced to live either with single parents or with multiple parents. Religious vision and commitment might help a spouse to be determined to save the marriage for the sake of the children, who are most vulnerable though they are identified in some religious traditions with God's image, power and love. While this is common for all spouses, interreligious marriage can present a distinctive situation in which such care is especially necessary from the pre-wedding stage to the wedding stages of their own children. In this section we will point out the commonality and difference in the perception of different religious communities with regard to marriage in general, and interreligious marriage in particular.

Hindus

For the Hindu, marriage is also a sacred institution whereby man and woman become one in spirit. Hindu marriage is also a social duty, and in the Vedic period it was a moral religious obligation as well. Marriage and the desiring for male children was the only possible way in which a man could repay his debt to his ancestors.[75]

Love, companionship, happiness, progeny and continuing the line of family and caste are normally mentioned in connection with the purpose of Hindu marriages. Monogamy is normal, yet polygamy is not unknown. The family and relatives normally understand if, on the ground of the first wife having no child, the husband takes another wife and it is difficult to ascertain the popularity of this practice as such 'additional unions' are not registered. It is again normal to choose the spouse within the wider family and caste although this is slowly breaking. Child marriage, once popular, is now very rare. Dowry is normally given to the groom and his family from the bride's parents. Match making in consultation with the concerned horoscopes is common.

In orthodox Hindu families (brahmanic or connected with brahmanic tradition) the wedding ceremony is regarded as one of the rites of passage (*samskara*). Apart from the centrality of the sacred fire and recitations and guidance of the Brahmin priests, the ceremony has the following four core elements:

1. Several oblations are made into the sacred fire.
2. The bridegroom takes the bride's hand, saying: 'I take your hand for happiness.'
3. He guides her three times around the fire. After each circumambulation he makes her step on a stone, saying:

[75] E. Turner and P.R. Frese, "Marriage", in *Encyclopedia of Religion*, ed. by M. Eliade, London: Macmillan, 1987, Vol. 9, 218.

'Tread on this stone. Be firm like a stone. Overcome the enemies. Trample down the foes.'

4. He makes her take seven steps toward the north-east, saying, 'Take one step for sap, two for juice, three for prospering in wealth, four for comfort, five for cattle, six for the seasons. Be my friend with your seventh step! May you be devoted to me. Let us have many sons. May they reach old age.' Most authorities consider these seven steps as the essential rite of matrimony; if the bridegroom dies before this rite is performed, the bride is not considered a widow.

   After the marriage rite the couple goes to the husband's home and remains chaste for three days. On the fourth day several rites are performed to ensure fertility, after which the marriage is consummated.[76]

In some ceremonies the gods and goddesses are invoked for granting boons and bestowing blessings. The divine couple (God and his consort) is viewed as providing a model and sometimes God's practice of having more than one wife is taken to justify one's practice of the same. The ceremony can be held anywhere – temple premise, home, hall. As far as the ceremonies of non-orthodox families are concerned, they are varied, and the simplest form is exchanging garlands and the groom tying a chain or thread around the neck of the bride in front of a priest in a temple or shrine. Where the ceremonies are held at home, a priest or the civil Registrar would be invited, although in rural areas continued encouragement needs to be given for proper registration of the marriage.

Parsis

According to the sacred texts of their religion which originated in Iran (Zoroastrian), 'marriage is divinely favoured'. 'The second happiest place in the world is that in which a righteous man set up his household.' The married pair is supposed 'to strive to live a life of righteousness and help one another in good deeds'. Marriage

---

[76] P. Olivelle, "Hindu Rites", *Ibid.*, Vol.12, 387.

is a religious duty and is held 'a meritorious act to help their co-religionists to enter the wedded state, and such assistance may even serve to atone for sin'.

It is by no means unusual, therefore, for Parsis to enjoin by will or by a trust that a certain amount of their wealth is expended in aiding poor brides to marry, and certain institutions, as the Parsi Panchayat of Bombay, provide special funds for this purpose.[77]

The marriage ceremony is preceded by several rites like fixing an auspicious day for the betrothal by consulting Hindu astrologers, the betrothal ceremony in which 'the women of the groom's family visit the house of the bride and present silver coins to her, and the groom receives a similar present from the women of the bride's family'. The older term of the ceremony is 'to name', 'since after the betrothal the bride receives in religious recitals of prayers for the name of the groom, even though, by some mishap, marriage does not take place. An un-betrothed girl was said to be "unnamed"... Betrothal is regarded as a solemn part of the marriage ceremony, the "pledge of the magnitude of a man" ...being considered...to mean a promise of marriage.'[78] The betrothal is followed by the lighting of a lamp early in the morning and an exchange of visits and gifts. The ceremonies are varied from country to country. The most common elements have the support of the scripture. Accordingly, in the morning or afternoon of the wedding day the bride and groom take a sacred bath. 'The religious portion of the wedding is usually performed shortly after sunset, perhaps to symbolise that, just as day and night unite and blend, so the wedded pair should be united in weal and woe.' Following a procession from the groom's place guided by the officiating priest to the bride's house where the ceremony is held, the groom receives a ceremonial welcome. An initial blessing is given.

The following requisites are necessary for a regular marriage: (1) the marriage must be celebrated before an assembly of at least five persons who have been summoned for this special occasion; (2)

[77] J.J. Modi, "Marriage (Iranian) 1. Zoroastrian", in *Encyclopaedia of Religion and Ethics*, ed. by J. Hastings, Edinburgh: T&T Clark, 1915, Vol. 8, 455.

[78] Ibid.

the contracting parties are asked by the officiating priest whether they consent to be united in wedlock; (3) the hands of bride and groom are joined, and a symbolic knot also plays a prominent part in the ceremony; (4) the actual marriage ceremony is followed by a benediction accompanied by sprinkling with rice, etc.[79]

Following the sprinkling of rice on them by the officiating priest the couple do it on each other. 'An egg, a coconut, and a little tray of water are now passed three times round the groom's head and cast away, and in the course of the evening the women of the bride's family make the groom dip his hand in a water-jar, in which he leaves for them a silver coin. Formerly it was also the custom for the feet of the bride and groom to be washed in the marriage ceremony, but the adoption of English foot-gear has caused this to survive only in washing the tip of the boots.'[80] There are more recitals and symbolic acts. At benediction God Ahura Mazda is invoked to grant them 'progeny of sons and grandsons, abundant means, strong friendship, bodily strength and long life'.

As far as the attitude of the Parsis to interfaith marriage is concerned there is nothing special, and what is said about Hindus applies to them.

Buddhists

Although, Gautama Buddha had to renounce his family and worldly pleasure for the pursuit of enlightenment, he came back to society with a new vision of life. The celibacy adopted by the early monks was the key for spiritual advancement towards *nirvana*, the ultimate goal. The laity and household life, however, was given due concern as they contributed to normal life in society. Right sexual conduct, chaste life, avoidance of adultery and warm-hearted genuine friendship are among the recurring ethical ideals taught by the Buddha. The Buddhist equivalent of showing reverence to the 'six quarters' provides a comprehensive vision of relationships in the family and society.

---

[79] Ibid., 456.

[80] Ibid.

The following should be looked upon as the six quarters. The parents should be looked upon as the east, teachers as the south, wife and children as the west, friends and associates as the north, servants and employees as the nadir, religious teachers and priests as the zenith.[81]

The Buddha explained the 'west' in the following way:

> In five ways, young householder, should a wife as the west be ministered to by a husband: (i) by being very courteous to her, (ii) by not despising her in any way, (iii) by being faithful to her, (iv) by handing over authority of domestic management to her, (v) by providing her with adornments.
>
> The wife thus ministered to as the west by her husband shows her compassion to her husband in five ways: (i) she performs her household duties earnestly, (ii) she is hospitable to the kith and kin of her husband, (iii) she remains strictly faithful, (iv) she protects his earnings, (v) she is skilled and industrious in discharging her duties.[82]

As far as the preparation for marriage is concerned much is like the Hindu and Zoroastrian pattern. There is no Buddhist wedding ceremony universally applicable. As Buddhism spread it took the customs of local areas and in conjunction with local cults. The Burmese style, which is very popular, is an example.

The wedding ceremony in Burma is not attended by Buddhist monks. This ceremony is a secular affair contained within religious rites. The Buddhist monks are fed a special meal in the bride's home the morning before the wedding. This feast acquires merits for the couple to be married and for the parents of the bride. A religious ceremony is held the evening after the wedding at the village shrine and offerings are made by the bride, her mother, and the mother of the groom to the guardian spirits of the village and to the spirit of the ancestors. During the secular wedding ceremony the couple are

---

[81] Quoted, H. Saddhatissa, *The Buddha's Way*, London: George Allen & Unwin, 1985, 105.

[82] Ibid., 105f; for a further elaboration see the author's and same publisher's, *Buddhist Ethics - Essence of Buddhism,* 1970, 133ff.

instructed to worship their parents and the Buddha. Their hands are held together and immersed in a bowl of water so that 'their union should be as indivisible as water.'[83]

Normally Buddhists are not bothered about the exactitude of rituals although in some areas the Hindu influence in this regard is visible. As in the case of Ananda of our earlier story, they are open to interreligious marriage if simplicity and meditation is respected.

Jains

Jain achievements in propagating the ideals of asceticism, non-violence and non-vegetarianism, through literature, iconography and architecture are due to 'the energy and courage of a comparatively united community'. Mahavira's beginnings, searching and organisation have much to share with that of the Buddha although their core visions of reality are different. Despite strong emphasis on celibacy, chastity and austere practices, the tradition provides teachings for a disciplined lay life in the household. The five great vows of non-killing, non-lying, non-stealing, non-attachment to worldly things and chastity which are strictly laid on the monks are simplified for the laity.

When it is agreed that a couple is suited, an *engagement ceremony* is held, to which prominent members of the community are invited; there is a ritual exchange of symbolic items and gifts and the engagement is recorded in an engagement document. This ceremony takes place in the home of the groom or in a community hall, and the date of the marriage is usually discussed at this stage.[84]

As far as the marriage ceremony is concerned, 'the correct rituals were lost for many centuries, and Jains appropriated a modified form of the Hindu marriage ceremony'. Consultations regarding the auspicious day and time precede sending invitations to the actual ceremony. Exchange of gifts takes place before and on the wedding day. The marriage ceremony is conducted by a Brahmin or by any well-respected Jain. Of the sixteen stages in the marriage

[83] Turner and Frese, Op.cit., 220f.

[84] Natubhai Shah, *Jainism: The World of Conquerors*, Brighton: Sussex Academic Press, 1998, 203.

ritual the most important are: invocation of heavenly goddesses in an auspicious ritual at the bride's home, similar invocation of gods at the groom's home, ritual worship in the temple for their wellbeing, the auspicious ritual at the home or wedding hall which 'invokes the gods of all places to establish the sacred place within which the wedding will take place', ceremonial procession of the groom and his party to the bride's home or wedding hall and a ritual welcome, auspicious prayers recited to certain gods and goddesses (after which 'the priest places a cloth garland around the couple's necks, and then the bride's parents symbolically wash the groom's feet'), uniting of the palms of the couple by the priest at the precise time deemed most auspicious and a series of invocation and offering with a view to ensure all blessings upon the couple, the couple circling the sacred fire four times in a clock wise direction, sprinkling of holy powder upon them by the priest and the final unclasping of their hands. 'In many cases, Jain weddings follow Hindu customs.'[85] The same can be said about their attitude to interreligious marriage.

Jews

Long history, varied locations of Jewish presence and difference of traditions followed have caused slight variation in practising marriage among the Jews. Basically, according to Jewish teaching, marriage serves three purposes: the propagation of the human species, mutual happiness in companionship and establishment of the family as a basic social unit. While the influence of traditional patriarchy continues it is overcome by progressive groups within the tradition.

Traditional material affirms the dignity of women and also encourages the enjoyment of sex. A husband is told to have thought for his wife's pleasure during intercourse. Sexual relations before marriage are strictly forbidden.[86]

Preparations for marriage include betrothal (traditionally a year before), fixing a day (any except the Sabbath and festival days) and purification bath of the bride by immersion. On the wedding day itself the couple fast until the ceremony. This takes place under a

[85] Ibid., 203ff.

[86] M. Braybrook, *How to Understand Judaism*, Albans Place: SCM, 1995, 33.

chuppah or canopy, held on four poles, which may be decorated with flowers. Although there are variations, a Jewish wedding takes a set form: initial blessing of wine and of the marriage, the ring, the marriage contract, the final (seven) blessings.[87]

When the bridegroom places the ring on the bride's finger he says: 'Behold, you are consecrated to me by this ring according to the Law of Moses and of Israel.' In the Progressive tradition the ring is reciprocated by the bride with similar words. These words have both religious and legal significance. 'The seven blessings link the couple with the story of creation, the history of Israel and its future hopes.'

For the main reason of maintaining lineage and communal solidarity, 'intermarriage of Jews with non-Jews (or Gentiles) is regarded as a significant problem'. This is in spite of such marriage taking place in more than fifty percent of cases in America and twenty percent in Britain. This often creates conflict between leaders of the two traditions, particularly the rabbis and Christian pastors. 'The response of some rabbis to this conflict between upholding Jewish tradition with integrity while also maintaining a positive relationship with the couple is to encourage them to be married in a civil ceremony and when, sometime later, their religious identity as a couple is established, to seek a blessing of the marriage in the chosen tradition. A Christian pastor troubled by the tensions for the faith community and for the couple in an interfaith ceremony, will find in her/his rabbinic colleagues sympathetic listeners as both traditions seek to maintain relationships with people without losing central aspects of the tradition, or neglecting real human tensions.'[88] When this involves non-Christians the tensions will of course be more severe.

Muslims

According to the Qur'an marriage is a sign that God created man and woman for a life of love, mercy and tranquillity between the couple (30:21). 'The prophet Muhammad said that marriage was half of religion and should be a guard for the chastity and morals of men

[87] Ibid., 33f.

[88] *Resource by Presbyterian Christians*, 13.

and women. Adolescents are taught to dress modestly and behave discreetly with the opposite sex and to defer sexual relations until marriage.'[89] Marriage is viewed to serve two purposes: production of and care for legitimate offspring and legitimisation of sexual relations. The right of the wife to financial and economic resources is also secured. In Islamic society the family is considered as the core which is secured by marriage. Article 5 of the *Declaration of Human Rights in Islam* published in 1990 states:

> The family is the core of society and marriage is the foundation of its civilization. Men and women have the right to get married, they may not be hindered by any limitations based on race, colour or nationality to exercise this right... Society and state have to remove all obstacles which prevent marriages and facilitate the conclusion of marriages. They must ensure the protection and the wellbeing of families.[90]

The Qur'an permits a Muslim man to have four wives provided he has the means to care for them and the mind to treat them equally. However, having one wife is the norm in most cases today.

Basically, for Muslims marriage is a social contract and a legal institution. They do not attach to it any dimension of sacramental mystery or sentiment of love as most Christians do. In many areas an engagement period is observed during which the spouses get acquainted with each other and their families. At the wedding a contract is formalised before the couple and two witnesses. The groom pays a 'bride money' (*mahar*) which secures her protection even at divorce if that is the case. The contract would mention all the conditions to meet with such an eventuality including religious training of the children, inheritance regulation and property settlement. Although, many Muslims take on board local customs, including a procession of the groom riding on a decorated horse, in the tradition no formal religious ceremony is required. Any Muslim of good standing can perform the contract. At the same time, religion

---

[89] Ibid., 14.

[90] Quoted, C. Lamb, *Marriage between Christians and Muslims*, 23.

is fundamental in the married life and the couple should be deeply conscious of God.

Marrying within the religious community is the norm in Islam. However, there is an allowance for a Muslim man to marry a Jew or Christian as they belong to 'the People of the Book'. In such cases the husband should respect and help his wife to practise her religion although the children are to be raised as Muslims. This allowance is not given for a Muslim woman and the reason given is the child having to adopt the religion of the father and possible harassment from the husband and his family. Some scholars think that this has no foundation. With regard to the religious adherence of one or both of the bride's parents and the nature of marriage (permanent or temporary) the Islamic law schools differ.

Christians

Christians in general take marriage as a natural and social institution yet 'a holy institution' as it was ordained by God at the beginning of creation. The Bible advocates 'mutual complementarity and perfection' between the couple and building up the family as partners in God's creation. We have already referred to the relevant biblical passages for establishing the theological and spiritual significance of marriage. In a wedding service, recalling those passages, describing the theological and spiritual significance, thanksgiving and prayer, readings from the scriptures, homily, exchange of rings or garlands or the groom tying a chain around the neck of the bride, the 'legal' declaration of the couple as husband and wife and blessing are the main elements.

Major Church traditions differ from each other in putting emphases in understanding the meaning and practice of marriage and in approaching interfaith marriage. The Orthodox Church considers it a mystery or sacrament in the sense it is 'an image of the mystical union between Christ and the Church'. It acquires ecclesiological and eschatological significance when as a sacramental act it 'sanctifies the natural institution of marriage and unites the partners in Christ into one flesh'. Through the blessing of the Triune God their family is transformed to a church and thus becomes an earthly unit of the kingdom of God. According to the Church canons interreligious marriage is prohibited. However, there has been increasing tolerance and permission provided the children are to be baptised and brought up in the Church. It depends on the benevolence of the local autocephalous churches towards their individual members. The Russian Orthodox Church is more positive in view of Paul's teaching about the possibility of a believer saving and sanctifying the spouse.

In the Roman Catholic Church also marriage is taken as a sacrament which signifies a covenantal love. 'In the divine consent, visible in the sign of blessing' in the liturgy for the celebration of marriage, 'the marriage partners sense their fellowship "before God" as an experience of salvation.' As long as living as a faithful Catholic Christian is not challenged, the Church allows its members to marry from members of other religions under certain conditions and the local bishop through *'express dispensation'* is authorised to deal with individual cases.

In the Church of England, the legally recognised position is that 'marriage may only be contracted between one man and one woman who are of an age to marry, who freely and publicly give their consent and who are not in law married to anyone else'. 'According to English law the Church of England is under the obligation to conduct marriages of all parishioners whether they are actually practising Christians or not, are baptised or not. At the same time, only the unaltered rite of the Church of England may legally be used. This means that people marrying in that church do not have to go to the Register Office prior to the ceremony. Other churches do not have this privilege, and a civil servant or registrar attends the wedding.'[91] Although this policy has been discussed several times, the 'established church' in England maintains this with a view to influence public opinion and ethos of married life. As far as interreligious marriage is concerned, the Church of England is very positive, and this is on the theological basis that marriage is a gracious and generous gift of God to all people.

---

[91] G. Chapman, *Catechism of the Catholic Church*, London: Cassell, 1994, 366.

The Church of England therefore refuses to serve only those already within its fold, without on the other hand compromising its witness. For many young couples the preliminaries and preparation for the church marriage are their first opportunity to acquire a more intimate understanding of what the Christian faith is all about. The Church hopes and prays that they may be touched and enriched by it. Marriage can often lead to a first or renewed commitment to the life of the Church.[92]

Thus because of its broad view of human society and the family and its missionary motivation, the Church of England has taken this peculiar position which is different from the Orthodox and Roman Catholic Churches on the one hand and the other Protestant Churches on the other, although many non-Anglican ministers of 'ecumenical' outlook will have equally 'broad' views. It is understandable then that more than any other Church, the Church of England is concerned about the pastoral issues involved particularly in interreligious marriage and the pastors are being equipped to deal with a variety of cases.

The Protestant Churches on the whole share the biblical and theological foundations of marriage adopted by the above Churches. The slight difference, however, is that they take it as a sacred institution but not a sacrament, at least in the technical sense. They would take the mystery mentioned in Ephesians 5:32 as in an Anglican interpretation 'that the unifying, self-giving, sacrificial love of man and woman in Christian marriage is an actual participation in the unifying, self-giving, sacrificial love of Christ in the Church'. One additional emphasis is on the sexuality being redeemed in marriage through transforming dominance of one partner into mutual subservience. Many Protestant Churches around the world recognise civil marriage as a God-given institution which is in line with national policies and government rules. For example, in India Christian marriage is governed by Christian Personal Law which is a special provision given in the Constitution, and Hindus and Muslims have their own personal laws. Ministers of every mainstream church like the Church of South India is authorised

---

[92] Ibid., 19.

to solemnise a wedding which is declared as both according to the will of God and the law of the nation. There are sectarian preachers and pastors who manage to obtain a licence from the government to solemnise marriage and they use it not only in their churches, but also, discreetly, in complicated cases of interreligious marriage. The Protestant Churches in India approve Christian marriage only between baptised members and that is the reason 'conversions for marriage' become very easy and popular. At the same time, there are churches willing to bless the civil marriage through a simple ceremony in the church and much depends on the courage and competence of a particular minister.

Sikhs

As a young world religion, combining elements of Islam and Hinduism, Sikhism has taken elements from both these traditions for understanding and practising marriage. The view of 'two bodies but one spirit' is found in the teachings of the cardinal gurus. The rite of engagement, if done, is performed in the presence of *Guru Granth*, the Sikh scripture. In this ceremony, after prayer and a reading from the scripture, the relatives of the girl present to the boy a sword and iron bangles as symbols of a dedicated life and some sweets. The marriage date is fixed by mutual convenience. The wedding ceremony, in normal Sikh worship in the Gurudwara, is centred in the scripture.

At the reception of the marriage party all sing prescribed hymns of welcome and joy and then prayer is offered. The marriage is solemnized in the presence of the *Guru Granth*. Any person from the congregation may perform it. The officiant, leading the prayer, asks God's blessings. The couple is told that they should become one in spirit. Four *lavans* (epithalamium) from the *Guru Granth* are recited and with the recitation of each *lav* the couple, bridegroom leading the bride, go round the *Guru Granth* and, before taking their respective seats, bow before the *Guru Granth*. The four *lavans* symbolise the four steps in the development of life of love: Fear, Love,

Restraint and Harmony. After offering the prayer of thanksgiving the prasad is distributed.[93]

Basically, Sikhs are tolerant of other faiths even though an element of heroic commitment on their part, because of the background of the origins of their tradition, is evident in their religious behaviour. For Sikh boys and girls to fall in love with members of other religious communities is not rare particularly among those who are educated and westernised. As they do not have a strong view of the proper manner of solemnizing an interreligious wedding, presumably it is left with the individuals.

The Baha'is

According to the Baha'is, as all religions are inspired by God they have to be tolerated and interreligious marriage is permitted. The Baha'i teachings on marriage see it as an eternal bond that survives past the lives of the partners in the physical life, and into the spiritual worlds. Thus, the teachings stress that during courting the partners must take the utmost care to become acquainted with each other's character. Furthermore, the husband and wife should be united not only physically, but also spiritually, so that they can improve the spiritual life of each other, and that they can spiritually advance towards God.[94] Engagement with the involvement the parents and a waiting period lead to the wedding. The Baha'i marriage ceremony is done differently in each culture. The only compulsory part of the wedding is the reading of the wedding vows prescribed by their prophet Bahaullah (1817-1892) which both the groom and the bride recite:

We will all, verily, abide by the Will of God.

This is to be done in the presence of two witnesses to be recorded through a Baha'i Local Spiritual Assembly. Legal recognition depends

---

[93] Raghubir Singh Tak "Rituals and Sacraments in Sikhism: A Sociological Perspective", in *Rituals and Sacraments in Indian Religions,* ed. by C.O. McMullen, Delhi: ISPCK, 1979, 128.

[94] https://en.wikipedia.org/wiki/Bah%C3%A1%27%C3%AD_marriage as on 23 June 2018.

on the civil laws of the country. Most Baha'i marriage ceremonies consist of the reading of Baha'i writings, prayers and music followed by a talk about the spiritual nature of Baha'i marriage, and then the reading of the vows.

A Baha'i ceremony should be performed with the non-Baha'i rite (or ceremony). If both ceremonies are performed, the non-Baha'i ceremony should not invalidate the Baha'i ceremony; the Baha'i partner remains a Baha'i, and is not adopting the religion of the other partner in the ceremony. The Baha'i partner should also abstain from vows (or statements) committing them to a declaration of faith in another religion or that are contrary to the principles of the Baha'i Faith. The two ceremonies should be performed on the same day; their order is not important. The Baha'i ceremony may be performed in the place of worship of the other religion if it is afforded respect equal to the non-Baha'i ceremony and is clearly distinct from the non-Baha'i ceremony.[95]

Services and Liturgies

Special liturgy for interreligious marriage is a topic known mainly among some Christian Churches and shared by Jews as well as Muslims. If it is truly interreligious liturgy, as we have suggested in the last chapter, it should be planned and prepared by an interreligious group as appropriate for the particular occasion. As the *Resource by Presbyterian Christians* puts it, 'For most Christian ministers, the preparation for a wedding ceremony for an interfaith marriage presents a great challenge. The Interfaith wedding service demands creativity and sensitivity.'[96] The ministers need to be equipped with a thorough understanding of marriage in different religious communities and sects, with dealing with couples for arriving at an agreed understanding of liturgy and its different elements and with co-operating with his colleagues from other faith communities. The *Resource* provides three sample liturgies. The first one is Muslim-Christian wedding liturgy. The call to worship ('In the name of God,

[95] See https://en.wikipedia.org/wiki/Interfaith_marriage#Bah%C3%A1'%C3%AD_Faith as on 23 June 2018.

[96] *Resource,* 37.

Most Gracious and Most Merciful...) is taken from the opening chapter of the Qur'an which is said in Arabic by the groom and in English by the bride. This is followed by an opening statement and prayer reflecting the gist of Christian and Muslim understanding of marriage. The other prayers and readings come from both the traditions. Pledges, vows and exchange of rings use secular terms and practice. The processional prelude, song before the benediction and recessional postlude remain as only titles. The benediction is from the Hebrew scripture, the Aaronic blessing ('The Lord bless you and keep you...).

The other two samples are from Christian-Jewish wedding liturgy. One has the order of opening words (about the biblical understanding of marriage), the promises, the exchange of rings, the declaration and the blessing which is Aaronic. The other has an entrance with a rubric of appropriate music and position of the couple and their families, sentences of scripture (Ps. 118:24, 26a), statement on the gift of marriage, prayer, declaration of intent, affirmations of the families, affirmation of the congregation, prayer and reading of scripture (Song of Solomon 2:10-14), vows, exchange of rings, prayer, announcement of marriage, charge to the couple and benediction (again the Aaronic blessing). If such weddings are possible between Christians and members of the non-Semitic religious tradition (e.g. Hindus) the liturgy can be much more colourful with flowers and incense and with many symbolic acts like mixed music and exchange of garlands as well as objects like banana bunches, coconut and sandal paste!

The above sample liturgies do not include a sermon or homily. Yet we have an excellent example of a sermon preached by Samartha[97] at a service of Blessing of a Hindu-Christian marriage in India. At the beginning he observed: 'Inter-religious marriages are not very common in our country. And yet they do take place with increasing frequency, that young people in love can break through barriers of religion and caste. In doing so, two families, two communities, two

[97] S.J. Samartha, *Pilgrim Christ*, Bangalore: Asian Tradition Corporation, 1994, 120-123 (Originally preached at St. Mark's Cathedral on 8 April 1985 at a service of Blessing of the marriage of a Hindu (bridegroom) and a Christian.

religions, and even two cultures have also been brought together.' Then he assured the parents of the Hindu groom, for whom presumably this was the first time to come near a Christian church, that 'the Christian Church, in essence, is not an exclusive communal body, but a fellowship in Christ where "strangers and sojourners can become fellow citizens in the household of God" (Eph. 2:19).' His brief sermon was based on two texts. One was 1 Cor. 13:13 ('So faith, hope and love abide, these three; but the greatest of these is love'). The other was a Vedic text the translation of which is: 'Faith is the wife, truth the husband at whose behest the sacrifice is performed. Faith and Truth: that is the supreme conjunction. With faith and truth combined one wins the heavenly abode.' Commenting on the Hindu and Christian scriptures belonging to the whole world and particularly on Paul's great poem on love he says:

> This love is divine because it is so human. It is human because it is so divine. It is particular because it is universal. It is universal because it is particular. Love is as wide as the horizon and as deep as the ocean. That is why human love, the love of two young people towards each other, can be so graciously accommodated within its depths.

With reference to the Hindu text Samartha pointed out its context saying that 'Husband and wife together participate in the sacrifice.' He made it a point to criticise the Christian practice of the father of the bride alone handing her over to the groom as if transferring a property from one hand to another. He suggested that 'We should either reject that part of the marriage service or both the father and mother should go forward.' He read in the combination of faith and truth in the text signifying the combination of wife and husband the message that they 'are asked to give their hearts to, and move towards that which is genuine and true'. He related this to the multireligious context of India where there is need for interreligious friendship and where 'the question of truth and falsehood can arise *within* each religion, but not always *between* them. We need to grow *together* in love and truth. Without love, truth can become harsh. Without truth love can become sentimental.' The absence of truth in the Pauline verse and of love in the Vedic text draw the preacher's attention and for him they were probably taken for granted. 'When the two texts are taken together,' he said, 'the love of truth is linked to the truth of love.' Samartha ended his 'Hindu-Christian sermon' with the words directed to the couple: 'May your marriage be a symbol and a sign of the future, bringing joy and happiness to you and mutual enrichment to two families, two religions and two cultures, as you move together in the pilgrimage of life.' This is a fine example of interreligious marriage providing an opportunity for interreligious understanding and communication in a profound manner.

Continued Support and Commitment

Samartha's sermon was very serious, striking profound ideas of faith and love. The studies we referred to earlier point out the seriousness of the pastoral role to be played in preparing the couple for interreligious marriage and in continuing a counselling service that will make for its endurance and enrichment. A report of a consultation on Islam in Europe defines the pastoral dimension in the following words:

> Pastoral theology is based on an evangelical awareness of faith, hope and love. It presupposes an in-depth awareness of socio-economic realities. It concerns every aspect, ad intra and ad extra, of the Christian community.[98]

One aspect mentioned is interreligious marriage. Pastors are advised to be alert to developments within such a marriage from preparation to even the end of marriage due to death of a partner or divorce. In any case they should be alert to the possibilities of any marriage within their pastoral jurisdiction in engaging with which they can use a range of resources, such as literature and counselling services, etc., both religious and secular. What is not clear in all these considerations, however, is the religious commitment of the couple who want an interreligious marriage.

The concern about the religious commitment can be within a particular religion. For example, Christians cannot claim that all those married in the church are committed to their faith. The *Resource by*

[98] Quoted, Lamb, Op.cit., 33.

Presbyterian Christians quotes from Elizabeth Achtemeier's book *The Committed Marriage* an assertion that 'Christian commitment and marital commitment are two sides of one dedication.'[99] Where the social dimension of religious life dominates the other dimensions, such as ethics and experience, a person can be respectfully nominal. Where religious adherence is identified with a political enclave, ethnic solidarity and cultural nationalism the chances of being nominal are more. Are there criteria to measure the level and depth of one's faith commitment except by making discreet observation and indirect comment? This is a challenge for any person or community that is serious about the particular vision and obligations of their faith. If this is the case within a faith community, is there any way to ensure serious faith commitment of the couple wanting an interreligious marriage?

The possibility of an interreligious couple bridging families, cultures and religions and thus profoundly practising interreligious dialogue is a wonderful idea. But while the opponents of interreligious marriage are one-sided in their evaluation (e.g. the salvific value of the religion of one partner), the exponents seem to be silent about the religious commitment of the couple. Is it only an issue for religious enthusiasts and fanatics? In the ecumenical discussions on dialogue we noticed an emphasis that real dialogue can take place only between people with commitments. What is not tackled or seriously recognised in such discussions is the fact of nominalism. The joint study document of OIRR/PCID makes an important note. From the viewpoint of Christian spouses it says that not much interreligious dialogue takes place within the household. 'Frequently *religious differences* are avoided or ignored.' As one of the issues for consideration, it states:

> It may happen that the partners will agree, either explicitly or tacitly, to eliminate all religion from their household. Religion is seen as a divisive element, and so is best avoided. It is not talked about, prayers are not said, the sense of belonging to the respective religious communities lost. Here, the result is a form of religious indifferentism.

[99] *Resources*, 9.

> Although, this is apparently the pattern of living of many couples and families in today's world, it should nevertheless be considered a loss. The marriage and family are deprived of the extra dimension religion gives to life. [100]

One significant difficulty for pastoral approach in such a situation is that an initiative taken by a particular religion's representative can be suspected and it can lead to further conflict also. Therefore, we should clearly distinguish between authentic ways of practising religion in total freedom and tendencies that strengthen nominalism or lead to it. Let nominalism and indifferentism not be mistaken for mutual tolerance and respect for all religions.

This is also true of political leaders who claim to represent a religious community. For example, in the recent history of the Indian sub-continent, we have seen numerous popular figures who represent religious communities but are themselves not religious. There are many such politicians in secular India who repeat the Vedic slogan of 'one truth and many names' for asserting an ultimate solution for the problem of religious pluralism. Likewise, a boy and girl may fall in love with each other and, for the sake of maintaining familial and communal bonds, want interreligious marriage. The responsibility of the Christian minister should not be reduced to organising a solemn wedding ceremony. He or she must be equally concerned about the faith and nurture of the couple. This is not to encourage one to convert to the religion of the other, but to make them aware of their qualification for having a wedding ceremony called interreligious. The opposite of religious nominalism is again not fanaticism, but commitment and openness.

If there is commitment and openness between the partners of a marriage there can hardly be any problem which is other than normal. In families in which such an atmosphere is maintained, the children also will grow with commitment and openness. Even if there is a dramatic change of religious allegiance, it will be taken in good spirit. If that happens as a result of genuine interaction and influence within a family who belong to a theistic tradition, as a way of responding to the particular manner in which the divine

---

[100] *Prog Dialogue,* 333.

grace was revealed, what they achieve is a profound union, union with the Creator and Saviour of the world. If they realise that this union is something different from and greater than a romantic and sexual union they have so far experienced, their witnessing life with all spiritual fruits will be natural. It is only those who have chosen to be indifferent to any such faith who can possibly criticise them for ending in this way.

The Roman Catholic Church is open in acknowledging the possibility of the couple becoming indifferent to faith and the desirability of the other spouse converting to become a Christian. The following catechetical clause reflects a warning as well as an expectation:

> Differences about faith and the very notion of marriage, but also different religious mentalities, can become sources of tension in marriage, especially as regards the education of children. The temptation to religious indifference can then arise... (quoting Paul's idea of a believer consecrating the non-believing spouse)... It is a great joy for the Christian spouse and for the Church if this 'consecration' should lead to the free conversion of the other spouse to the Christian faith. Sincere married love, the humble and patient practice of the family virtues, and perseverance in prayer can prepare the non-believing spouse to accept the grace of conversion.[101]

One can easily point out that 'family virtues', 'perseverance in prayer' and 'believing' are not exclusive traits of Christians. There may be cases that the non-Christian spouses are more serious about them. Then it can be a challenge to the Christian spouse to rediscover the foundations of his/her faith if he or she realises that faith has been nominal or misguided.

What is most important for those involved in providing pastoral support, particularly Christian pastors, is to help safeguard full religious freedom of the Christian spouse and rediscover or grow in faith. Compared to the studies and resources available on Christian

[101] G. Chapman, Op.cit., 366.

marriage and pastoral counselling, both intra-church and inter-church, materials on interreligious marriage are less than minimal. Those who encourage and promote interreligious marriages need to think of producing materials with details of all important aspects of such marriage touching even the delicate issues of emotional stability and expression as well as sex in marriage. There may be contexts where cultural issues interplay with religious practice in the family. For example, in India a considerable number of Christians are called 'secret Christians'. In a country where freedom of religion is a fundamental right, for maintaining familial bonds and cultural cohesion, open expression of their faith is curtailed. While affirming their faith and commitment, pastors and Christian leaders need to consider their case far more seriously than now. What should be accepted almost as an interreligious creed is that only in a creative space of open interaction between committed couple in a family context the truth of religion will shine in its splendour which will encourage more young people to come forward for interreligious marriage with clarity and confidence.

On the whole, interreligious marriage raises profound questions about the compatibility of opposite human sex beyond religious affiliations. There operating is faithfulness to each other which could be a common human value. But what is not clear is whether there is a commitment on the part of one partner to knowing the religious vision and persuasions of the other. If love is the key, they should explore its depth together and its authentic manifestation in the life within the family as well as in the society. Such examples will help others to appreciate interreligious marriage and potential partners to approach it both positively and seriously.

Chapter 5

Interreligious Funeral

Common End and Community Bond

Death is one of the most common human realities, and yet there are different religious perceptions of it and different beliefs and practices attached to the funeral. In a multireligious community every funeral in a sense is interreligious. It is one of the occasions in which without waiting for special invitation members of a community come together out of respect for the deceased and solidarity with the bereaved. However, those standing around a graveyard or gathered in a prayer hall are not automatically aware of what is going on in a funeral ceremony or service. And, strictly speaking, a funeral cannot be called interreligious unless it is arranged by an interreligious team and done according to more than one religious rite as per the will of the deceased or the wish of the dear ones. In this sense it is very rare to see interreligious funerals in ordinary contexts. At the same time, the topic is significant as it can draw attention to a most sensitive part of human life and to the particular ultimate goal held by a religious community.

Some sort of interreligious funeral does take place in extraordinary contexts. In India, for example, when a political leader is dead and being buried or cremated, apart from the main ceremony appropriate to his/her religious adherence or ideological persuasion, different religious communities are well represented in singing/chanting and praying. Famous social activists also draw together such interreligious gatherings and the offering of songs and prayers. At the international level certain funerals bring world leaders together. Such moments can provide a moving experience, which are not only politically significant but also spiritually edifying. The funeral of Gandhi in January 1948 is a good example. A later example is the funeral of Yitzhak Rabin, a former Prime Minister of Israel, a military commander turned peacemaker, who was assassinated in a peace rally by a right-wing Israeli in November 1995. His funeral attracted a few notable Arab leaders, who were normally considered his political enemies with religious overtones. It was observed in the press that he won their affection and confidence more at his death than while he was living. In both the above cases, however, the primary rites performed were Hindu and Jewish respectively. We can add many stories of tragic deaths that move people and funerals that motivate them for a new life of awareness of human life and reconciliation.

Studies on the funeral as one of the rites of passage prevalent among different religious communities, both ancient and modern, from anthropological and phenomenological perspectives, abound and the published materials are numerous. But they do not show any interest in exploring a viable form of interreligious funeral. Likewise, more than any other religious communities, Christians have before them ample materials on funerals. An acceptable interreligious funeral service, however, has yet to emerge. Interestingly, sometimes Christian sources expose a hidden assumption that what is acceptable for Christians is applicable to people of all religions. For instance, a major volume is entitled 'Human Rites– Worship Resources for an Age of Change', having us believe that it deals with the funeral and other rites of all religious traditions, but in fact it deals with only Christian rites, and there is no mention of others.' It exposes an attitude among Christian writers and publishers, which is not untypical. The last item of this compiled work, thankfully, is a prayer which is fascinating:

> Go-between God, in-weave the fabric of our common life, that the many-coloured beauty of your love may find expression in all our exchanges.[102]

There is much that is inspiring in this prayer for a Christian attending a Hindu or Jewish or Muslim funeral, inviting members of other religious communities for a Christian funeral, or exploring the possibility of producing an interreligious funeral service. It is of course not like preparing an interreligious worship liturgy in general or interreligious marriage liturgy in particular because, as we have already noted, deliberate arrangements for an interreligious funeral arevery rare, again depending on the will of the deceased or wish of his/her kith and kin.

Beliefs and Practices

Where an actual interreligious funeral does not take place, but the presence of members of the different religious communities is evident, it is important to know the beliefs and practices related to a funeral among different religious traditions. It will help not only to respect strange forms of ritual behaviour, but also to have fruitful dialogue about their meaning and about the ultimate goals of human life with members of a particular religious community. Some people think that what matters is accepting birth and death as inevitable parts of common human life and that there is no point in discussing about meaning of rituals and ultimate goals. But those who take their faith and others' faith seriously would like to know why particular acts are included in a funeral. A scholarly essay on funeral rites starts with the following observation:

> Death is not only a biological occurrence leaving the corpse as a residue that must be administered to; it is also, and more importantly, a socio-cultural fundamental because of the

[102] H. Ward & J. Wild (Compiled), *Human Rites: Worship Resources for an Age of Change*, London: Mowbray, 1995, 320.

> belief and representations it gives rise to and the attitudes and rituals it brings about. It is of course understood that rites are the immediate extension of beliefs, and that funeral rites, in particular, are the conscious cultural forms of one of the most ancient, universal and unconscious impulses: the need to overcome the distress of death and dying.[103]

Is this distress overcome by only one way? Of course not. A brief consultation of the funeral rites of some major religious communities will elucidate this point.

Hindus

The funeral, for Hindus, is the last of the rites of passage. Starting from the Vedic practice which continues mainly in brahmanic circles, the funeral pyre provides a person with the opportunity of a third birth, the first being the natural birth and the second birth achieved by an initiation ceremony which qualifies them for Vedic learning. It is one's last sacrifice also, as it culminates all the ritual sacrifices one performs in one's lifetime. Just as the flames of sacred fire take up the oblation to heaven in ritual sacrifices, the funeral flames of cremation take up the sacrificer himself (or herself) to the abode of gods and ancestors. According to the original vision, the person will enjoy the life of this abode until the merit accumulated through regular performance of sacrifice on earth gets exhausted. Then an idea of 'second death' developed, the logical conclusion of which was the idea of the transmigration of the soul according to the accumulated merit of one's action in the previous birth (*karma samsara*). Action, both ritual and moral, liberative knowledge and devotion to God were proposed by different streams of thought within the Hindu religious traditions as alternative or progressive ways of final release from the bond of the chain of births and deaths. Whether one is sure of the stage of liberation at the time of one's death is not openly expressed.

[103] L-V. Thomas, "Funeral Rites", in M. Eliade, *Encyclopedia of Religion*, Vol. 5, 450.

While those traditions (e.g. the Vaishnava) continue to do the funeral in the Vedic manner, there is no common way of doing it which can be termed 'Hindu'. Traditions and regions differ from each other in their practice. For instance, the regional devotional sects use chants and recitation of their distinctive texts. In some areas the dead body is positioned sitting on a bier decorated with flowers and carried on public roads with the kith and kin drumming, dancing, shouting and fire-cracking. Offering food to various spirits including those of the ancestors, professional mourning, making presents to the survivors by their close relatives, shaving of their heads by the sons of the deceased, spraying the ash in sacred rivers and the sea and the sprinkling of water brought from sacred rivers like the Ganges are some of the auxiliary practices. There is difference in minute details between various caste-groups.

Buddhists

According to the Buddha, the present life is part of a dynamic process of 'dependent origination'. Yet he taught that humans must think of death, for it is inevitable and can stimulate thinking about the nature of human life. He advocated for the monks a meditation on the process of dying, on the dead body and on the process of the body decomposing. The monks were encouraged to attend to a dying person even in the rainy season. There are certain ceremonies to quieten the spirit of the dying. The ceremony includes music, flowers and perfume so that all the five senses of the dying are occupied by their influence.

Buddhist funeral rites are varied, and the Hindu influence and incorporation of local customs are evident. The following is the most popular practice in Southeast Asia:

> The only life crisis solemnised by monks is death...Monks must officiate at funerals; there is always a sermon, and the preacher is given cloth to use for robes, a surrogate for the shroud which was originally declared suitable stuff for a monk's robe. Death rites do not end at the funeral. The bereaved family must subsequently invite monks to be fed and to preach, and transfer the merit to the newly dead,

> in case he has been reborn as a hungry ghost (*peta*) who can only accomplish good (and so hasten to better life) by empathizing with this merit.[104]

It is believed that the fire which consumes the body is able to ignite life in new body with the continuing soul unless the state of *nirvana* is already attained. The feeding of monks, a substitute for Hindu practice of feeding the priests, will continue after a period of seven days, then three months and then annually.

Jains

The Jains share the Hindu belief in transmigration of the soul causing the rebirth of even the highest gods. In explaining the operation of the karmic force and in holding the view of the ultimate goal of the soul, i.e., a state of pure consciousness, however, they are different. Self-mortification and euthanasia ('wise death by starvation in case of incurable illness', or in the case of those *arhats* who have attained liberation) are accepted in the tradition.

'When Jains visit someone who is dying, whether at home or in a hospital, they sing hymns and recite the *Navakara Mantra.* A dying person would like to receive, during this crucial period, forgiveness for any wrong committed to others during his or her life, and to forgive all who have done wrong to him or her, and to have a peaceful death. If the dying person cannot chant, someone else will substitute so that the dying person has noble thoughts, and the soul leaves this world in a peaceful state.'[105] After death, there is recitation of mantras and hymns and incantation of the ancient 'conquerors' of the tradition until the body begins its journey in a procession towards the cremation ground. 'The body is placed on the funeral pyre of logs of wood or sandalwood and covered with more wood; it is then sprinkled with ghee, incense and flammable materials. A close relative makes three circuits of the pyre, chanting mantras before

---

[104] R.R. Gombrich, "Buddhist Cultic Life in Southeast Asia", Ibid., Vol. 15, 466; for the case of Theravada school see Gombrich, *Theravada Buddhism*, London: Routledge & Kegan Paul, 1988, 124f.

[105] Natubhai Shah, *Jainism: The World of Conquerors*, Brighton: Sussex Academic Press, 1998, 207f.

lighting it...After the body is consumed, the participants in the funeral ritual return home, bathe and purify themselves by chanting mantras. It is customary that women do not take part in any of these rites.'[106] For two days there are consoling acts by the community and repeated periods of hymns and narrative stories emphasising the Jain philosophy. 'On the third day, the ashes are taken and thrown into a nearby sacred river, but if there is no river nearby, they are put into a pit, thus the physical body composed of the five material elements returns to its origin. It is believed that the aura of the sorrowful atmosphere of the deceased's house remains for three days, but it alleviates with the benefit of special prayers, hymns and peace recitals, resulting in a gradual normalisation of the bereaved family's life. The third day ends with a visit to the temple where donations to worthy causes are made, but some observe the period of sorrow for the deceased for up to thirteen days, when temple worship or puja is performed in the presence of community members.'[107] Necessary modifications are made in the above rites to suit the convention and convenience of Jain migrants living outside India.

Parsis

Death and disposal of the dead are dramatic events among the Parsis. When death approaches, one or two priests are invited to perform the ceremony of confession that might lead to repentance so that the departed soul goes to heaven without any obstruction. Pouring the consecrated *haoma* juice and dropping a few grains of pomegranate into the mouth of the dying is considered meritorious.

The body is washed and covered with a clean but worn-out white suit of cotton clothes and the sacred thread is tied round. The corpse is placed on a clean white sheet on the ground of the prepared spot in the house. Two relatives sit either side in contact with the body 'forming a bridge for the soul'. The corpse is unclean and defiling and therefore the two relatives are soon replaced by two consecrated funeral-servants. 'The face must not be turned towards the north, whence the demons proceed.' Special dogs are brought

[106] Ibid., 208.

[107] Ibid.

near to scare away the corpse-demon; so also, the demon-killing fire which is fed by sandalwood. The corpse-bearers remove the body on an iron bier in daytime exposing it to the sun. Led by a man bearing a fire-vase, the procession includes priests, relatives, carriers of the corpse and priests. After paying last respects at the entrance of the 'Silent Tower' (built in a separate ground), the naked corpse is left in the middle of the open central well of the tower. The waiting vultures scavenge by eating up the flesh and leave the bones for the slow decay. There are filters fixed so that no element of the corpse pollutes the earth. Prayers are offered at each stage of the event. And after the disposal there is a ceremony at home which includes the sprinkling of cow-urine throughout the house.

Jews

Family and friends are expected to stay with the dying person among the Jews. The rites of mourners, i.e., father, mother, brother, sister, son, daughter and spouse, are clearly defined. There are three periods of mourning: from death to burial, the seven days following burial, from the end of the seven days until the thirtieth day. Mourners are forbidden to engage in pleasurable activities such as drinking wine, eating meat and sexual intercourse. As soon as a person is dead the eyes are closed, the jaw tied up, arms and hands kept straight and accessories removed. The body is usually disposed of as soon as possible. The body is wrapped up in a plain linen cloth, and normally a male is buried with his prayer shawl. Burial in a simple wooden coffin is the norm among the orthodox Jews, but the Progressive groups do not mind cremating. There is a Jewish burial society to arrange the burial. Several psalms are recited during the ceremony starting from washing the body and the completion of the funeral. The Jewish belief about death is reflected in the following memorial prayer which is offered at the funeral:

> O God full of compassion, you who dwell on high! Grant perfect rest beneath the sheltering wings of Your presence, among the holy and pure who shine as the brightness of the heavens, unto the soul of...[the deceased] who has entered eternity and in whose memory charity is offered.

> May his/her repose be in the garden of Eden. May the Lord of Mercy bring him/her under the cover of his wings forever and may his/her soul be bound up in the bond of eternal life. May the Lord be his/her possession and may he/she rest in peace. Amen.[108]

The Jewish emphasis on equality of human persons is expressed in the funeral by not only referring to the biblical verse 'for dust you are and to dust you shall return', but also not allowing to show one's wealth and fame at this solemn moment.

Christians

Christian funerals share elements of the other Semitic traditions of Judaism and Islam, but the variety of elements and practices are more among Christians according to denominational emphasis and local customs. The Roman Catholic Church declares:

> For the Christian the day of death inaugurates, at the end of his sacramental life, the fulfilment of his new birth begun at Baptism, the definitive 'conformity' to 'the image of the Son' conferred by the anointing of the Holy Spirit, and participation in the feast of the Kingdom which was anticipated in the Eucharist – even if final purifications are necessary for him in order to be clothed with the nuptial garment.[109]

Although, 'the Christian funeral confers on the deceased neither a sacrament nor a sacramental', the Catechism notes that it is 'a liturgical celebration of the Church. The ministry of the Church aims at expressing efficacious communion with the deceased, at the participation in that communion of the community gathered for the funeral, and at the proclamation of eternal life to the community.'

'The Order of Christian Funerals of the Roman liturgy gives three types of funeral celebrations, corresponding to the three

---

[108] Quoted, P.S. Knobel, "Jewish Rites" in *Encyclopedia of Religion.*, Vol. 12, 396f.

[109] Chapman, *Catechism of the Catholic Church*, 375f. 9. Also see Ibid., 376f.

places in which they are conducted (the home, the church and the cemetery), and according to the importance attached to them by the family, local customs, the culture and popular piety. This order of celebration is common to all the liturgical traditions, and comprises four principal elements. These elements are the greeting of the community, the liturgy of the Word, the eucharistic sacrifice and a farewell to the deceased.'[110] All or most of these elements are woven into different forms in different Orthodox Churches and Protestant denominations.[111] Burial is the popular practice in most traditions, but cremation is increasing in urban western societies 'as a hygienic and space-conserving process'. In fact, a Christian funeral may be bewildering for attendants from other religions unless the particular denomination's way of doing things and emphases in the services are clearly explained.

Muslims

Funeral ceremonies are almost the same throughout the Muslim world. Continuous reciting of the Qur'an gives assurance of life after death for the ailing person who is expected to die. As in the Jewish custom, at the point of death the limbs of the body are set in position. The face of the deceased is turned toward Mecca, the central holy place of Islam. Regular social life of those close to the deceased is suspended during the mourning period. An expert is called in to wash the body and prepare it for burial. The body is wrapped in a white seamless cloth, and in the case of those who have made the pilgrimage to Mecca, thus fulfilling one of the five religious duties of Muslims, the same garment used during pilgrimage is worn. Burial takes place as quickly as possible. The bier is simple and the body is covered by a green sheet and friends and relatives accompany the silent procession. A religious specialist recites a prayer at the cemetery. Participants in the procession are provided a meal at the house of the deceased on returning from the cemetery. The mourning period continues for three days. The Muslim emphasis on submitting to the will of God

---

[110] Ibid., 376f.

[111] For different ways in which the burial is done in various church traditions, see "Burial" in Davies, *A New Dictionary of Liturgy and Worship*, 117ff.

finds expression in the way the community maintains composure after the initial shock of their beloved one having departed although feeling of sorrow is expressed in indirect ways.

Sikhs

According to the legendary biography of the Hindu-Muslim saint Kabir of the fifteenth century, a forerunner of the formation of Sikhism, the Hindu-Muslim conflict was reflected in the competing claims of two armed parties of his followers over his dead body. When they opened the tent to which he had retired they saw nothing but a heap of flowers which was divided between them. The Muslims buried their share on the spot and erected a cenotaph over it and the Hindus cremated their share and built a memorial tomb at Benares.

Understandably, elements in Sikh funerals come from both Hindu and Islamic traditions. Just like the Muslims, the Sikhs maintain composure at the time of death submitting it to the will of God. Historically, thirty years after the death of Guru Amar Das (1574) it is said that his grandson, Sundar Das, when requested by Guru Arjan (1581-1606), the fifth cardinal guru, 'wrote an account of the instructions which Guru Amar Das left regarding the ceremonies to be performed at the time of his death. The account was accepted by Guru Arjan.' Accordingly, the funeral takes place as quickly as possible, mostly on the same day as the death.[112]

The dead body is washed and clothed by members of the family. If the deceased belongs to the order of 'Singhs', the body is dressed with the five symbolic objects: uncut hair and beard, a comb, a steel band, shorts and a sword. After the offering of prayer. The body is taken to the cremation ground. With prayers and chants the body is placed on the pyre. The ashes and bones are thrown into the nearest river. The relatives and friends join in a final prayer and after reading from the scripture the sacred food (*prasad*) is offered. The bereaved family continues to read the prescribed portions of the scripture for ten days.

---

[112] See Joginder Singh, "Rituals and Sacraments in Sikhism: A Historical Perspective" in McMullen, Op.cit., 94.

Baha'is

In terms of death, the Baha'i faith teaches that there is a separate consciousness or soul for every human. Upon death, the soul is relieved of physical bonds and enters the spiritual world, a timeless extension of the universe. Spiritual development determines whether one is closer or farther from God.

Baha'i funeral customs and practices do not permit embalming unless it is required by law. Cremation is also not permitted. The Baha'i faith does not prohibit donation of the body to medical science.

The body is prepared by washing and wrapping in a white shroud. A ring with the inscription 'I came forth from God, and return unto Him, detached from all save Him, holding fast to His Name, the Merciful, the Compassionate' should be worn. The body is then placed in a coffin for interment. Traditional practices require that the body be buried within one hour's travel time from the place of death. It is felt that this discourages people from becoming attached to any particular geographic site. There is some flexibility in calculating where the limit is, but the important thing to keep in mind is that the spirit of the faith's teachings is that you should be buried near the place of death.

Baha'i funeral services are normally held within two or three days after the death. Guests may dress according to personal preference and local custom. The family arranges for the officiant to read the prayers. One key requirement for a Baha'i funeral is reading of the Prayer for the Dead.

Baha'i funeral customs do not discourage non-believers from attending or being present when the Prayer for the Dead is read. If non-Baha'is are attending a Baha'i funeral, they should keep in mind that this is a sacred tradition and be appropriately respectful during the reading.[113]

In a multireligious community, in general, members naturally come to know the customs and rites of the funerals among their neighbours. Where there are friends from outside, it is always useful to orient them to the distinctive practice in any particular case so

---

[113] https://www.funeralwise.com/customs/bahai/as on 23 June 2018.

that they can, without unnecessary apprehensiveness, participate in the funeral. It is unfortunate that while books repetitiously abound containing the history and concepts of our different religions, most of them do not include the rites of passage in any detail. Particularly, the funeral rite is the most neglected. Those who are involved in the ministry of interreligious dialogue must address this situation by bringing out booklets explaining the ritual performed in rites of passage like funerals. Where there are distinctive customs of a local type they should be mentioned very clearly.

Interreligious Funeral Service

Interreligious funerals in the strict sense of the term are very rare, as we have already noted. If there is a will from the deceased or wish of the close relative, preparing an interreligious funeral service is not more difficult than preparing interreligious worship in general and an interreligious marriage service in particular. There can be an agreed order of service, including prayers, chants and readings, from the religious traditions concerned. It should be emphasised again that if it is really going to be an interreligious funeral, Christian ministers should avoid rushing into dominate the arrangements, using their expertise of having done Christian funerals. Perhaps, the very word 'funeral service' is very much a Christian product and others may not share its wordy nature. Funeral rites in other religious traditions have several symbolic acts as we have noticed. Therefore, there should be an agreed understanding of how many such acts are included in a particular funeral service.

What will most probably be desired by way of an interreligious funeral is not a multi-religious funeral but a bi-lateral service where ceremonies can take place in two separate ways or together. Ariarajah, as part of describing an issue of mixed marriage that continued even after the death of a partner, mentions a story told by a minister, his colleague in Sri Lanka. A Hindu had married a Christian woman. 'Even though the man never accepted baptism or officially became a Christian himself, he allowed his children to be baptized and had regularly attended the church with the family. When the man died, the wife wanted to give him a Christian burial. But his brothers and sisters insisted that he should be cremated according to the Hindu rites because he had never converted to Christianity or accepted baptism as a mark of it. They could not come to an agreement, and my colleague had to come up with the compromise that the body be first cremated, then he would preside over an act of burial of the ashes!'[114]

Samartha has reported a Hindu-Christian funeral held in Bangalore. The deceased was a Hindu and his wife Christian. The family wanted a Hindu-Christian funeral held in one son's house in an afternoon. Samartha himself was asked to say a few words and offer a prayer. He describes the scene as follows:

> There was quite a large gathering at the service. He had many Hindu and Christian relatives and friends. Some of them had come from places as far away as Calcutta and Delhi, Cochin and Mangalore. They were all sitting together in the gathering. No one tried to behave like a theological porcupine or a spiritual jellyfish. They were all human beings drawn together in the common bond of grief.[115]

In his speech, Samartha mentioned that the deceased was a committed Hindu who happily lived in the fellowship of a Christian family. In his prayer he made use of an Upanishadic reference to Ultimate Reality as 'that from which everything is born, that by which everything born is sustained, and that into which everything returns at the end'. Since it was a Palm Sunday he 'referred to the journey of Jesus who started his journey from the Father, and was now returning to Him by way of the cross and the resurrection'. Further, he 'affirmed that, at the moment of death, our faith and hope as Christians are grounded in Jesus Christ, the crucified and risen Lord. The prayer was unmistakably Christian in content and character.'[116]

---

[114] W. Ariaraja, *Not Without My Neighbour*, Geneva: WCC Publications, 1999, 86.

[115] Samartha, *Pilgrim Christ*, 126.

[116] Ibid.

Christians had their service first, in which Jesus' words 'I am the resurrection and life...' were affirmed. Two Christian ministers were present. 'The order of service of the Church of South India for the occasion is beautiful and moving. The whole architectural construction with hymns, readings and prayers, has spiritual depth, theological strength and pastoral comfort. It was a clear affirmation of Christian faith and hope in God through Jesus Christ.'[117]

The Hindu friends then took over. Another Upanishadic verse was referred to in which it is said that in the world of heaven there is no fear of death, old age, hunger, thirst and sorrow but joy. 'On the right side of the body, near the head, was the broken half of a coconut with a bit of camphor burning within it. On the left, was a brass vessel with water from the Ganga river and leaves from tulsi (a plant sacred to the Hindus). An earthen pot with glowing coals was at the foot of the body.'[118] Usually, the eldest son of the deceased officiates at a Hindu funeral ceremony, 'but in this case, since his son was a Christian, the eldest son of the sister of the deceased, who was a Hindu, took over the leadership. All this was done without the slightest bit of argument or confusion or hesitation.' 'The Hindu friends slowly walked around the body in a dignified procession. Usually women do not take part in such ceremonies. But in this case (Samartha noticed that) women and children were also in the circle. Each one took some tulsi leaves and put a few drops of water into the mouth of the body, folded hands in the *namaste* gesture, and touched its feet. They were quiet, solemn, and moved with a sense of rhythm. No Hindu priest was present nor were any mantras recited.'[119] The rest of the funeral, including carrying the body on a wooden plank to the crematorium, was shared by both Hindu and Christian friends. Samartha remarks on the difference between a Christian funeral and a Hindu funeral, of which the former is formal, wordy and rigid whereas the latter informal, full of symbols and symbolic acts. As far as the religious view of death is concerned, he says that 'When it is believed that there is only one life there is more pressure and anxiety

---

[117] Ibid., 127.

[118] Ibid.

[119] Ibid., 130.

at death than when it is accepted that there is a plurality of births and deaths, offering more opportunities for the individuals to realise his or her destiny.' Of course there are those who argue that it is precisely because of this view that Hindus are less enthusiastic and radical in trying to change the present condition of the individual and society, and that the poverty, untouchability and corruption that mar the life of 'Hindu India' would speak volumes about this fact.

Samartha ends his report and reflection with some penetrating questions which echo the spirit of some of the speculative hymns of the Hindu scriptures (Vedas) and of the sceptical sayings of the Bible's Ecclesiastes.

> Can one body, in the utter helplessness of death, carry the weight of two religious rites? How will the destiny of the person be affected by this on the other side of death?
>
> Can the same body be claimed by two religious groups, Hindu and Christian? Why not? Was he not related to both Hindus and Christians biologically and spiritually?...
>
> Is it not strange, even tragic, that life should separate religious people but that death should bring them together, even for a brief moment?
>
> Did he live as a Hindu and die as a Christian? Or did he live as a Christian and die as a Hindu? Who knows?[120]

No one can answer these questions easily, nor do we dare to answer them here! Nevertheless, these questions can form a basis for an open discussion on the ultimate destiny of humanity as viewed and believed within different religious traditions. And if interreligious funerals cannot encourage such a discussion they are not seriously religious but lifeless occasions of fulfilling a social expectation and paying respect to the departed. The following section is meant to give clues for the worth and importance of such discussions.

---

[120] Ibid., 130.

Living Faiths and Ultimate Goals

However much we experience an elation of the spirit and even devotional ecstasy, religious people everywhere face fundamental challenges of life. Funerals may stimulate thought about the meaning and goal of life. Sudden awareness of impermanence, of fleeting moments of pleasure and of hitting the feeling of nothingness or apparent disappearance of all hope and confidence push humans to ask questions about the nature and destiny of life. And inexplicable illnesses lead people to feel nervous, distraught and depressed. Phrases like 'the dark night of the soul' and 'terrifying experience in the abyss' give only glimpses into what people really experience and express. There are devotees of God who mourn separation from their Lord and long for reunion. In such and more situations religion offers hope for the possibility of a new or better life here and now, as well as for some sort of life after death – its form depending on different belief systems. They may, for example, present the view that love is as deep and mysterious as death, and as high as the heavens. It is extraordinary indeed that those who profess a religion and practise it celebrate victory in the face of failure and life in the face of death.

Samartha edited the book *Living Faiths and Ultimate Goals* (1974). The essays of this volume reflect on the understanding of 'salvation' and the ultimate goal of human life in Hindu thought and life, in the Buddhist view of *nirvana*, the Jewish understanding of redemption, the Christian meaning of salvation, the Islamic view of unity and alienation, the Marxist view of liberation, the salvation history of new China, the Christian-Marxist struggle for liberation in Latin America and in the African experience of salvation today. The scope is so limited that ideas from Jaina, Parsi, Sikh and Baha'i traditions could not be included in this book. Yet, one may marvel at the variety of ways human beings have perceived their ultimate destiny. There is no common humanity as far as the ultimate goals are perceived in different religious traditions. Samartha concludes his 'Introducing the Discussion' with the following words:

> To be open to God cannot mean prejudging the mind of God and erecting our own neat lines of demarcation as

> if we knew just where the Spirit of God is and is not at work. He is not bound by our prejudging. Nor is it to abandon commitment to the Truth as this has become known to us. It is, rather, gratefully to acknowledge that the fullness of Truth is always wider and deeper than our present apprehensions of it and that the Spirit is at work, in ways such that we do not know where He comes from nor where He is going, to guide us into all the Truth.[121]

Obviously, as a Christian minister and theologian, Samartha speaks in Christian terms. These terms may not be applicable to the other religious traditions. This is true not only for the quasi-religious traditions like Marxism which aims at achieving the goal of a classless society in which finally the State will wither away, but also to Buddhism which holds nirvana (or *nibbana*), an unexplainable state, as the goal. In the Hindu religious traditions there are different visions of which the most popular one in the advaita Vedanta is unification with or absorption into the ultimate reality or Supreme Soul and inseparable union with God in the heavenly world. In the devotional traditions (e.g. Saiva and Vaishnava), liberation from the bond of the chain of births and deaths is a common precondition in all the traditions and the divine grace in some form breaks it. Jains define nirvana as a state of pure consciousness, and Sikhs share the visions of Hindus and Muslims. Parsis (Zoroastrians) believe in a joyful life in paradise.

The Semitic traditions have many things in common. All of them believe in the final judgment of God and everlasting life of joy in the heavenly world. The criteria for the Jews is obeying the commandments of God as given in their scripture and interpreted in the tradition and for the Muslims submitting to the will of God as it is defined in the Islamic law. The distinctive reference in the Christian belief is to Jesus. After affirming the universal presence and work of God, Paul said in his speech before the Council of Areopagus at Athens:

[121] Samartha (ed.), *Living Faiths and Ultimate Goals*, Geneva: WCC, 1974.

> God has overlooked the age of ignorance; but now he commands men and women everywhere to repent, because he has fixed the day on which he will have the world judged, and justly judged, by a man whom he has designated; of this he has given assurance to all by raising him from the dead (Acts 17:30,31).

At the same time, truth requires us to admit that there is no blueprint in the Bible about life after death but the vision of a fuller life of intimacy with God, Christ and God's children is unambiguous. 'Dear friends, we are now God's children; what we shall be has not yet been disclosed, but we know that when Christ appears we shall be like him, because we shall see him as he is' (1 John 3:2). Even after attending an interreligious funeral, if we need not 'abandon commitment to the Truth as this has become known to us' as Samartha suggests, and if the unbound Spirit does not fail to refer to and glorify Christ according to the New Testament witness, how do we proceed to discuss on ultimate goals with people of other faiths?

We need not start with ultimate goals but with what we can do to improve the present life, many would say. There is much credibility in this position. Ecumenical discussions on interreligious dialogue emphasise that while we continue to dialogue on ultimate goals or suspend them for a while, as members of different religious communities, let us work with the proximate goals of achieving 'justice, peace and integrity of creation'. This is, indeed, most desirable, and we need to know more about attempts of this kind around the world and about the discussion that has ensued from them. In some of our experience, though, it is very clear that questions about ultimate goals need not be suspended at all because for many the vision about the ultimate end alone can give meaning and succour to work for improving the present in co-operation with people of other religions and secular ideologies. Those who believe in *karma samsara* (the chain of births conditioned by actions, ritual and moral) may try to improve their next birth by doing service for others. Jews and Muslims take the law and commandments of God which have to be obeyed and they include injunctions for doing justice and mercy for others. For a Christian the coming glory of the kingdom of God which is described in various ways in the scriptures is a motivating factor to work for the transformation of the present world with selfless love. Members of other small religious (popular) communities might also come forward to work together with similar motivating visions. For the Baha'is, there is no such physical place as heaven or hell but the eternal journey of the soul towards perfection. They explain that names like heaven and hell are symbols. For them the true reward is being illumined by the *radiance of the sun of reality and endowed with all the fine virtues. The opposite is the reward of the evil and wicked.* And authentic dialogue takes place between such people who work for improving life in the present yet are aware of the ultimate destiny of human life. Serious participation in an interreligious funeral can provide an unparalleled opportunity for such working together and sharing one another's vision for the future.

On the whole members of different religious communities in interreligious gatherings are either shy of or maintain a strategic silence about expressing their hope for the ultimate end. One major reason is that they are carried away by the modern trend created by secular liberal thinking, scientific and technological development. But all over the world there is a counter trend to question the ultimate meaning of human life and to rediscover the 'soul'. There was an interreligious seminar on 'The nature and Destiny of (Hu) Man' held at TTS in Madurai. In his reflective report of the seminar, R. Srinivasan, Principal and Professor of Education at Gandhigram (university), made the following observation:

> (Hu)Man has been more concerned with material benefits than a genuine desire for understanding himself (herself). Advances in science and technology have boosted his (her) ego and he (she) is perhaps strengthened in his (her) belief that he (she) can, one day, become the master of all that he (she) surveys. Yet, now and then, the discerning eye can spot cracks creeping in his (her) personality integration. With increased automation and growth of mass societies, he (she) is frequently haunted by a lurking fear of isolation,

> alienation and anonymity. We see him (her) subjected to constant pressures, for the sake of efficiency and success, to assume compartmentalised lives. With a surfeit of material prosperity and creature comforts, he (she) is developing restlessness and is challenged from within to face fundamental questions about the nature and meaning of life.[122]

One may point out that genuine inner aspirations and restlessness can well be covered over and casual conversations can be superficial and artificial, as is all too apparent in the secular ethos of the modern world.

Another reason for not talking about ultimate goals publicly is the dubious way in which certain religions developed ideas to suit the vested interest of some of their custodians. For example, according to some religious traditions, killing and being killed in a 'righteous war' ensures an easy passage to heavenly life. The ugliest development of this view is killing in the name of God as we see in the activities of a few terrorist organisations with a religious identity. No person who is truly committed to genuine interreligious dialogue can justify such activities, and most surely condemn them as destroying the image of the religious traditions concerned. For we all affirm life and respect it.

Christian behaviour in a secular and technocratic culture is equally ambiguous. By repeating their creeds in worship services Christians affirm Christ's coming to judge the dead and the living and the life everlasting. However, many have chosen to do charity and social service for others while keeping totally silent on their vision of the ultimate goal of life. This is well reflected in the watchword of the UK charity Christian Aid, 'We believe in life before death.' Does it not indicate indirectly that, therefore, we have no concern about people who fear death and the importance of life after death? Does belief in resurrection after death for an eternal life of total intimacy and equality as Jesus affirmed necessarily contribute to neglecting the life and wellbeing of life here and now? I am not

[122] R. Srinivasan, R. 1973: "Dialogue on the Nature and Destiny of Man – Some Reflections", *South India Churchman*, August, 1973, 8.

here arguing in favour of one at the cost of the other. As we have already pointed out, our conscious vision of an ultimate goal need not divert our attention from working for changing the present; on the contrary, we work for it with full vigour, joy and confidence for the sake of realizing the ultimate vision and goal. It is true that a number of Christians are individualistic and other-worldly in their understanding of salvation. But, strangely, they are not opting out of the world following the model of the desert fathers and monastic mystics whose influence on the ideal of self-denial in the history of the Christian church was considerable. For that matter several Buddhist monks around the world are living examples of such self-denial. What we see today is a strange combination of a prosperity doctrine and pious demonstration. Taking the parable of Jesus about the rich man and poor Lazarus who reached opposite ends at their death, these people seem to twist its meaning by wanting to be like the rich man in this world and Lazarus in heaven! In any case their hypocrisy and worship of mammon under the cover of a cross do not go unchallenged. Nevertheless, in fear of being identified with the inward-looking and other world-oriented Christians, should we be silent concerning the biblical vision for a glorious life after death in continuation of what we experience here in this world? Even the recognition of the supremacy of love, which finds expression in our relation to God and fellow humans in all its splendour and depth, leaves its logical end to be realised in the life after death. As Paul mentions in his great poem on love, 'At present we see only puzzling reflections in a mirror, but one day we shall see face to face. My knowledge now is partial; then it will be whole, like God's knowledge of me' (1 Cor.13:12).

When the context of an interreligious funeral provides a reference or opportunity to discuss living religions and ultimate goals, the participants in the discussion need to be open to say boldly what they really believe and listen patiently to what others have to say. Difference of opinion in each tradition and community needs to be acknowledged. In what way the ultimate goal relates to our pressing obligation to work for the development and transformation of the present world, both separately and jointly, should be a fruitful sharing. We will elaborate this in the next chapter. No one should prejudge the mind of God or the Ultimate Reality and dictate the divine will. God is Most Merciful, All Compassionate and Supremely Loving. The Buddhist and Jaina vision of the Ultimate Reality has the integral values of kindness, compassion and harmlessness. The joy and confidence with which we look to the future hope of humanity does not qualify us to become judges nor to run a Registry to reserve souls for that life after death. However, we have every right to be advocates of what we believe in and hope for and witness to the love of the Almighty which cannot be separated by death or by our funerals.

Belief in heaven and hell is connected with some other questions as well. Humans are moral beings sensing accountability for their actions related to their personal, familial and social life. Many do not accept the capricious and inhuman nature of mere chance producing the fruits or rewards of their actions but believe in a Supreme Being accounting for this process who is both loving and just. How does a compassionate, gracious and merciful God deal with humanity, including devotees, is a question asked, with answers suggested in various theologies. Also, the idea of God's judgment and punishment of the wicked gives some solace for the victims and vulnerable people of this world. Pushed to a corner by oppressive and exploitative forces, they lament and even curse the other with the words 'Let God see to you!' They proclaim that God is watching the criminals of the underground and those who conspire against the innocent with their power and influence. Moreover, they imagine a heavenly world above for the righteous and a world beneath for the unrighteous. In some traditions there are stories of gods and ancestors descending and ascending, thus giving an assurance of the ultimate victory of justice and love.

The plurality of visions of after life (e.g. heaven and hell) and their qualifications and passages is both complex and fascinating. It is normal to judge all others within the framework and scale of one's own religion. Openness to the possibility of a plurality of the scales may be possible. Paul, in the context of conflict of opinions between Jews (who insisted on observance of the law) and Gentiles (that is not indispensable in the new framework of divine grace) suggests the following: God judges all with justice particularly using the scale of

Jesus (Acts 17:31). But no one can judge others (Rom. 2:1). Further he says:

> And all who sin apart from the law will also perish apart from the law, and all who sin under the law will be judged by the law. For it is not those who hear the law who are righteous in God's sight, but is those who obey the law who will be declared righteous. (Indeed, when Gentiles, who do not have the law, do by nature things required by the law, they are a law for themselves, even though they do not have the law. They show that the requirements of the law are written on their hearts, their consciences also bearing witness, and their thoughts sometimes accusing them and at other times even defending them). This will take place on the day when God judges people's secrets through Jesus Christ, as the gospel declares (Rom. 2:12-16).

Though the context is parochial and the framework (Jesus Christ as judge) particular, there is an insight to understand the criteria of judgement. Accountability and specific focus on ethical life is held in every religion and secular ideology. For those who believe in one God or automatic operation of a moral law, a generous outlook is possible. This can be extended to the secular value systems which are professed as whole or accepted selectively, as propagated through the mass-communications. However, all these can be limited to individual life. But living in an interreligious context, the desired proximate goal seems to develop a collective will and to initiate engagement in a perplexing world.

Chapter 6

Interreligious Engagement

Ecumenical Shifts

As we noted in the first chapter, it was evident in the first World Missionary Conference 1910 that in Christian mission a new approach was necessary to people of other religions. The report/book entitled *The Missionary Message in Relation to Non-Christian Religions* represented a new shift in mission among people of other religions. It provides an assessment of major religions, recognising their strengths and weaknesses. The Christian message had to be shared with respect and courtesy. There was encouragement for Christians to study other religions with certain amount of objectivity. However, there was overall missionary optimism to 'evangelize the world in this generation'. But World War I (1914-1918) shattered the optimism as the main players in the war were from the so-called Christian countries.

The second WMC held in Jerusalem in 1928 focussed on the ill effects of spreading secularism and the need for world religions to respond jointly. Although, there were individuals reading and reflecting the different versions of secularism and political experiments, there was no organ to mobilise a common interreligious front to confront secularism. And even the idea was upset by the third WMC held in Tambaram, Madras, in 1938 where the domineering voice was for a radical theological discontinuity with other religions as they had been human-made whereas Christianity had the witness to the divine revelation, the only revelation. The local attempt of 'Rethinking Christianity' stressed on indigenous expressions of Christianity and the re-conception of the Christian message. However, though the nationalist movement for independence of India was moving to a climax and people from different religions participated in it, the Rethinking group made no efforts to mobilise interreligious awareness about the consequences of the struggle for the wellbeing of all in future. At the same time, World War II (1939-1945) shattered the missionary optimism again.

Following the war, strenuous efforts were made to establish unity in the church and in the world. The title of the volume, *Renewal and Advance*, which embodied the record of the missionary conference at Whitby, Ontario in 1947, indicates its dominant mood. The call was to go forward with 'renewed courage, and in the confidence that the world was eager to hear the gospel'. 'Expectant Evangelism' was one of the two distinctive slogans of the meeting; the other was 'Partnership in Obedience'. The context of partnership was still the missionary task in the 'non-Christian world.'[123] The next meeting at Willingen, Germany in 1952 set as its task 'a profound rethinking of the nature of the missionary obligation of the Church.' Even though it was realised that the 'Church-centric mission' of the past had come to an end and that 'mission belongs to the very being of the Church itself', both were simultaneously affirmed. There was no serious consideration of the religions of the people who were mainly the targets of this mission. However, one remarkable outcome of the Willingen meeting was the creation of 'Regional Study Centres', some of which later promoted interreligious dialogue

[123] L. Newbigin, "Mission to Six Continents", in *A History of the Ecumenical Movement - vol.II*, ed. by H.E. Fey, Geneva: WCC, 1986, 177.

in their regions. The Christian Institute for the Study of Religion and Society, Bangalore (1956) was one of them. Forging interreligious relationship and facilitating dialogue was one of its activities from the beginning.

While the shock of the War combined with fascination for humanist and secular thinking caused the start of disenchantment from religion in general and Christianity in particular, the World Council of Churches was formed in Amsterdam, Netherlands 1948. Its first General Assembly reflected on human disorder and God's design. 'The Approach to Other Faiths' was discussed. In the report of the section, which was received unanimously by the Assembly, whilst acknowledging that much in God's purpose 'is still hidden from us', three things, it was asserted 'are perfectly plain'. They are: (i) All that we need to know concerning God's purpose is already revealed in Christ. (ii) It is God's will that the Gospel should be proclaimed to all people everywhere. (iii) God is pleased to use human obedience in the fulfilment of his purpose.[124] At the same time, in its description of 'The Present Situation' the Report mentions that:

> The millions of Asia and Africa, filled with new hope, are determined to seize now the opportunity of shaping their own destiny...
>
> The word *faith* has acquired a new context. For most men*[sic]*, it is faith in the new society, now to be founded once for all, in which the 'good life' will be realised...In face of many religions and philosophies, it is held all truth is relative, and so the necessity of a costly personal decision is evaded.
>
> The religions of Asia and Africa are being challenged and profoundly modified. In the period of transition, the minds of millions are more than usual open to the Gospel.[125]

---

[124] W.A. Visser't Hooft (ed.), *The First Assembly of the World Council of Churches*, London: SCM Press, 1949, 64.

[125] Ibid., 65.

One can see that the pendulum was swinging back and forth from strong commitment to preach the good news on the one hand, and on the other being open to people of other religions for sharing friendship and working together for the common cause. One also notices this throughout the activities and discussions in the various units of the WCC. Most remarkably, Stanley Samartha, who was appointed as Associate Secretary in the Department of Studies in Mission and Evangelism, was made responsible to pursue the study on 'The Word of God and the Living Faiths of Men' and to co-ordinate the work of the study centres related to the Division of Commission on World Mission and Evangelism. Since then, development was rapid and far reaching, taking new directions and effecting new structures. A proper approach to people of other religions became one of the indispensable questions in discussion on mission as evident in the deliberations of the Assemblies of the CWME. At the same time, interreligious dialogue soon gained its distinctive identity through the creation of a new sub-unit within the programme structure of the WCC in 1971. Since then almost every program unit of WCC could not but relate to the question of relating to people of other religions. Particularly, the General Assembly of Nairobi 1975 proved to be controversial on the question of interreligious relations as we saw earlier; the report presented was titled 'Seeking a World Community', a community of communities and pluralistic cultures with creative mutuality. This was a radical shift from earlier emphasis on world mission and the formation of church as an exclusive community to witness to the gospel of Christ by word and action.

The 1982 *Ecumenical Affirmation on Mission and Evangelism*[126] prepared by CWME and adopted by the Central Committee of the WCC, reflects the WCC thinking on mission before forthcoming General Assembly, Vancouver 1983 and, interestingly, consolidates the perceptions and issues on interreligious dialogue that had emerged since Edinburgh 1910. For instance, within the framework of the missionary obligation of the church, both by words and service, it

[126] Published with co-operation of the Division of Overseas Ministries, National Council of the Churches of Christ in the U.S.A., New York, 1983.

affirms God as the creator of the whole universe and insists that he has not left himself without witness 'at any time or in any place', and the Spirit of God as being constantly at work 'in ways that pass human understanding and in places that to us are least expected'. In entering into dialogue with others, therefore, it states that 'Christians seek to discern the unsearchable riches of God and the way he deals with humanity.' It also speaks of 'encountering of commitments', mutual witness and 'spirit of openness and trust'. The San Antonio Conference on World Mission and Evangelism, 1989, the first of its kind since the integration of International Missionary Council (established in 1923) with WCC in 1961, came up with similar affirmations.[127]

We have already discussed the meaning of dialogue within interreligious relationship and the limited value of the word dialogue. It was left to the Christian leaders of Asia to point out with such a force. In the Seventh Assembly of the Christian Conference of Asia at Bangalore in 1981 stated:

> As a matter of fact, we are not quite satisfied with the term 'dialogue', as it gives the impression of mutual interchange of ideas and beliefs more on the intellectual level. We need a more suitable word which can convey the sense of mutual co-operation between people of living faiths and ideologies in coping with social evils in concrete measures for building truly human communities.[128]

In the subsequent consultations and documents including that of bilateral encounters, interreligious cooperation for nation building and social transformation was increasingly emphasised. The distinction between proximate goals and ultimate goals which could be parallel concerns of dialogue became a slogan; so also mobilising

---

[127] See F.R. Wilson (ed.), *The San Antonio Report*, Geneva: WCC, 1990. Particularly see Report of the IVth section on "Towards Renewed Communities in Mission" (68-79); plenary presentations on "Gospel and Culture" (122-124) and "Christian relationship to people of other great religious faiths of humankind", 124-126.

[128] Quoted, A.J. Van der Bent, *Vital Ecumenical Concerns*, Geneva: WCC, 1986, 59.

religious resources for social change. Consultations were held on this theme. For example, a consultation held at Rajpur, North India in 1981 brought together for the first time representatives of Christians and Hindus from areas of the world where people of these two religious traditions live together in great numbers. They included theologians, philosophers, spiritual leaders, pastors and social workers. The theme was "Religious Resources for a Just Society". The Hindu idea of *dharma* was expounded in a comprehensive way covering all aspects of a liberated life and life in its fullness which would parallel the Biblical vision of *Shalom.*[129] But there were no models of concrete action suggested to realise the visions of Shalom and Dharma.

To round up from Edinburgh 1910 to Edinburgh 2010, the concern for interreligious cooperation for the common good has been growing consistently. In preparation for the centenary celebrations there were consultations on different themes. A consultation on interreligious relations was held in UTC Bangalore and the outcome was a statement on 'Together for Life'. This was reflected in the overall report, entitled 'Together Towards Life: Mission and Evangelism in Changing Landscapes –Proposal for a New WCC Affirmation on Mission and Evangelism' (submitted by the Commission on World Mission and Evangelism, 5 September 2012). The dialogue theme is introduced as follows:

> The church lives in multi-religious and multi-cultural contexts and new communication technology is also bringing the people of the world into a greater awareness of one another's identities and pursuits. Locally and globally Christians are engaged with people of other religions and cultures in building societies of love, peace and justice. Plurality is a challenge to the churches and serious commitment to inter-faith dialogue and cross-cultural communication is therefore indispensable. What are the ecumenical convictions regarding common witnessing and

[129] See *Religious Resources for a Just Society: A Hindu-Christian Dialogue*, Geneva: WCC, 1981.

> practising life-giving mission in a world of many religions and cultures? (no. 9)

In detail, it is acknowledged that

> … in the plurality and complexity of today's world, we encounter people of many different religions, ideologies and convictions. We believe that the Spirit of Life brings joy and fullness of life. God's Spirit, therefore, can be found in all cultures that affirm life. The Holy Spirit works in mysterious ways, and we do not fully understand the workings of the Spirit in other faith traditions. We acknowledge that there is inherent value and wisdom in diverse life-giving spiritualities. Therefore, authentic mission makes the 'other' a partner in, not an 'object' of mission. (no. 93)

It further states:

> Dialogue is a way of affirming our common life and goals in terms of the affirmation of life and the integrity of creation. Dialogue at the religious level is possible only if we begin with the expectation of meeting God who has preceded us and has been present with people within their own contexts. God is there before we come (Acts 17) and our task is not to bring God along, but to witness to the God who is already there. Dialogue provides for an honest encounter where each party brings to the table all that they are in an open, patient and respectful manner. (no. 94)

Other affirmations in the document include

> the common creation, the universal presence and act of the Spirit, dialogue as 'a mutual encounter of commitments', dialogue of life and action, the spirit of dialogue and 'an attitude of respect and friendship', sharing deepest convictions and listening to others, and being challenged and enriched by others, freedom of religion particularly for minority religious communities, contribution to common

> good and that 'Followers of all religions and beliefs have equal rights and responsibilities.' (no. 95-96)

On the whole, the document reflects the shifts, ups and downs of the ecumenical movement over a century, particularly in relating the evangelistic mission to interreligious dialogue. The struggles, dilemmas, repetitions and guidelines point out the continuing concern of most of the Protestant churches worldwide. However, the words and thoughts come from the experts and the experienced. It requires a special study to assess their impact on the ordinary Christians around the world, particularly those who are conservatives and fundamentalists. The above is a Christian speech from the high galleries of the ecumenical movement. Since 1975, representatives of other religions have been observers and guests in many meetings, but it is not evident about their impressions and attempts to initiate similar reflections in their religious organizations and communities.

Some National and Local Situations and Experiments in India

With or without any connection with the ecumenical emphasis on interreligious cooperation, some rare individuals and groups have initiated remarkable discussion and action in India. Indian history is not less bloody than many other histories. Most remarkably, Bengal was divided by the British rulers into two in 1905 – East Bengal with a Muslim majority, and West Bengal with a Hindu majority. Since then Hindu-Muslim tension with occasional outbursts of violence have strained the relationship between these two communities. Despite all efforts, the partition of India-Pakistan at Independence in 1947 could not be prevented. And during the exchange of people across the two countries violence erupted and more than one million were massacred. For many the wounds are still bleeding. But it was not the end of the conflict. No one expected that the number of Muslims who opted to remain for practical and emotional reasons would be more than those who went out to Pakistan. Hence continuing tension, and voices for similar separation by the Sikhs. Christians appeared to be an introverted and nervous minority although their service in the areas of education and health were appreciated. Soon with the influence of American fundamentalism, groups emerged in India and in the name of evangelism they were often noisy, divisive and irritating.

Paul D. Devanandan (1901-1962), the first director of the CISRS (Christian Institute for the Study of Religion and Society), did some research on the Hindu concept of *maya* (false appearance!) and, with the support of the views of the modern Hindu thinkers, interpreted it as meaning the positive reality of life. To view the world as illusory as held by one section of the philosophical Hinduism, he argued that there was at least then the urge to change it. On the other hand, those who take the world positively come forward to transform it. He connected this to the Christian position that in the coming of Jesus Christ a new creation was inaugurated.

Devanandan viewed that since a new creation and a new age is already the present reality, and since God is a God who works actively in history and is relational, it is important that Christians are involved in peace making, nation-building and actively participate in acts of social transformation. Devanandan stressed that serving people (i.e. in education and health) was part of the Christian obligation and it should never induce people to become Christian. But he never compromised on exercising the duty of sharing the Christian message with appropriate re-conception. He thought that it was possible for committed Christians to give service or technical advice as 'non-professional missionaries.'[130] He also felt that young Christians should be willing to serve the nation and the people through engaging in political activity. He observed that 'the Christian minorities have a distinctive contribution to make to the development of the nation of Southern Asia through political participation.'[131]

Devanandan felt strongly that Christians need to watch more closely the issues of minority rights, religious freedom and undue governmental regulation of the lives of citizens. In relation

[130] P.D. Devanandan, *Christian Issues in Southern Asia*, New York: Friendship Press, 1963, 118-119.

[131] Ibid., 120.

to social reform in Asian context he found, 'people dislocated from their traditional life by the impact of world forces, becomes a genuine concern and they required social reform. So, the total social structure has to be reconstructed in terms of human rights and social justice.'[132] He also felt that increasing food production, land reform and population control in Asian countries are some of the important concerns. In all these, he advocated that 'Christian Churches are called to give positive guidance in these matters not only to their own members but also to other people.'[133] It also can help to educate public opinion in regard to problems like public health, leprosy and tuberculosis. He asked Christian leaders to be aware of the problems and struggles of the poor and labourers. The Church should not neglect them but should be actively involved in the process of developing community.[134]

Through the CISRS, Devanandan and his colleagues pioneered in organising programmes of interreligious dialogue. Research projects were initiated. Their journal *Religion and Society* carried articles on the emerging independent India. As a well-acknowledged ecumenist and thinker, Devanandan was invited to give the keynote address in the WCC's third General Assembly, New Delhi in 1961. He called Christians to be witnesses in their local areas by engaging in transforming activities. As there were pessimistic notions such as fate and pre-destination he asked them to be signs of hope for the glorious future.

CISRS was an inspiration for the theological seminaries in India to take up interreligious dialogue and to engage in socio-political reconstruction. As we noted earlier, the Tamilnadu Theological Seminary (established in the temple town of Madurai in 1969) started a Religious Friends Circle in 1977. Contact with visiting Muslims and Hindus was cordial. One Hindu professor lived in the seminary campus teaching in the local university while teaching part time in the seminary. His presence facilitated informal conversation in the safe context of community life. Visit to temples, mosques and

[132] Ibid., 125.

[133] See Ibid., 128-129.

[134] See Ibid., 133-134.

spiritual groups in and out of Madurai brought opportunities to widen the horizon of knowledge about people and their religious life.

While ecumenical discussions on interreligious cooperation for social change was initiated, Dayanandan Francis, the leader of the RFC, me as its organiser and a few other friends were keen on initiating creative and concrete action as an expression of interreligious relationship. How long do you go on meeting and talking while a great number of people around us are suffering from avoidable causes? This question was raised in a one-day seminar arranged on behalf of the RFC in 1978. Interreligious co-operation for social change was the theme. At the end of the seminar a decision was made to engage in practical co-operation in a noble cause. The menace of the growing number of beggars in Madurai was pointed out. The authorities of temples, mosques and churches allowed beggars to sit in front of them asking the devotees for alms. If we took responsibility for all the beggars at one stroke it would be unmanageable! Therefore, it was decided to concentrate on those beggars who were lepers too. The decision was to establish an interreligious rehabilitation home in Madurai and to run it by trustees from all the three religions. Even at the initial discussion some Hindus pleaded for the exemption of those wandering beggars who have religiously dedicated themselves for that life. The Muslim friends were unanimous in stating that no Muslim can be a beggar as Islam prohibits begging. An allowance for such sensitive cases was approved. Representatives from the three communities who were members of the RFC were asked to work out the detail. Subsequently, the location for the proposed home was chosen and appeals for financial contribution were sent. The only contribution received was from a Roman Catholic priest. Some Hindu friends whispered to us, to our great embarrassment, 'You have congregations to mobilise support, but we don't, and you have overseas contact too.' Some Muslim friends said, 'You are experienced in doing such works.' Some members even appeared to be hesitant to continue membership of the RFC. Therefore, the plan was abandoned. It was modified as a day care centre for those beggars-cum-lepers willing to go to a place attached to a Christian hospital. It was a learning experience for understanding attempts at interreligious co-operation for common concerns.

Then there was a positive experience. Unexpectedly, I had a rare chance of meeting Baba Ampte in April-May 1988 along with a team of the Student Christian Movement of India for whom I was supposed to be the Bible study leader. It was a work camp organized by Ampte to dig contours for bringing water from one place to another in the District of Chandrapur, Maharashtra. In the scorching summer heat (48°C) the work started early in the morning and breakfast was served in the site, and we came back for lunch and then to the tent where hundreds of young people from different religions shared fellowship with arguments and spells of laughter. Most memorable was interreligous conversation while digging. My Hindu partners were amused to know that I was a student of the Bhagavad Gita and currently engaged in a research on the Gita's views on Vedic sacrifice. In one afternoon they organized a session with me that proved to be the most useful encounter I ever had.

Meeting Baba Ampte (1914-2008) itself was an enriching experience. His first question to me was why Christians build tombs while they believe that Jesus rose from the dead by breaking the tomb? First, I did not realize that this question had a concrete background. His amazing experiment of *Anandvan* (Happy Forest) was then a huge commune run by leprosy patients for leprosy patients with attached institutions including four colleges. The development had a fascinating story. Maharashtra had the highest concentration of leprosy patients in India. Ampte, a freedom fighter and Gandhian, lawyer by qualification, then a mayor in Nagpur, being moved by the plight of the leprosy patients, resigned his job, went to Calcutta with his wife and two boys, got trained in a leprosy home, and came back with five leprosy patients. He approached the government who gave a piece of 7- acres of barren land and, when they found water, that was expanded to about two thousand acres of land. They claimed to be able to produce anything except electricity and kerosene oil! Those cured of leprosy were encouraged to go back to their villages, equipped with tools and the necessary means to start a new life. The other option was to remain members of the commune and work as assigned. There were a few kitchens and dining areas. When someone died there was the community support, and the burial place was a garden and on the spot of every burial a new tree was planted.

Ampte was a remarkable man. His physical impediment (he could not sit, therefore he had to either stand or lie down to give a speech) could not diminish his vigour and his smile. While he respected the Hindu *bhakti* of his wife, he appeared to be a humanist with the strong influence of Gandhi and Jesus. In their hospital, there was a photograph of a cross with Ampte's words: 'I cannot carry the cross, yet I try to go under its shadow.' For him, searching for God or soul was a futile exercise, and in a suffering brother or sister one could find both! There was a room full of his awards but he hardly visited them. When Prime Minister Indira Gandhi visited him, his condition was that she should go to his place as a free person without any bodyguards. She signed the visitors' book noting that she wanted to see such development everywhere in India. I came away not only with a shirt cloth made there but also with the vision that a tomb can be replaced by a tree or plant. Environmental concerns were integral to Ampte's vision of social reconstruction, and his two sons are said to continue to live and work with this vision with a special focus on environment and wild life.

In a recent study, along with Ampte, four other Indian environmentalists are listed.[135] They do not overtly belong to particular religious communities. Even if they are wrongly identified with a community that is often by religious fanatics. They demonstrate that their spirituality is of a higher order thus releasing remarkable energy creatively for the good of humanity and the natural world. At times they have to fight with vested interests exploiting religious identity. They have not spent their time and energy to write a secular critique of religion as is done in the West. For them if some are inspired by their visions and traditions to work for the liberation of the weak and vulnerable there is no problem as long as it is not trumpeted. Such examples should inform and inspire interreligious cooperation for social reconstruction.

---

[135] Medha Patkar of Narmada Bachao Andolan, Mylamma of the anti-Coca-Cola campaign, C.K. Janu in solidarity with tribal labourers, and Binayak Sen who was wrongly identified with Maoists for his involvement with the peoples' movement. See W.S. Annie, "Environmental Spirituality" in *Religion, Spirituality & Secularity in Multi-Religious India*, ed. by I. Selvanayagam, New Delhi: Christian World Imprints, 2017, 141-157.

To be Sensibly and Credibly Religious

Public criticism of the hypocrisy of religious life and action might unnerve people with religiosity and religious adherence, and consequently they may hide in their burrows. At the same time, there are those who argue for the due place of religion in a morally confusing and socially perplexing world. Earlier voices for creating a religion-less world have not been appreciated for various reasons. What will replace religion? Is religion irredeemable? There is great scope for interreligious communities, particularly leaders and scholars to engage in dialogue and come up with convincing answers.

No one has denied that religion or a sense of the sacred has been integral to human life, as is evident in history. When the taboo against approaching religion with freedom and critical outlook was transgressed in the 19th century by the translation and study of scriptural texts, a flurry of activities erupted in the academic world. Many theories and analytical tools were invented. However, no scholar has claimed to have any convincing definition of religion, either as a feeling or an activity. A survey of hundreds of definitions proposed by scholars would reveal that it is inconclusive, and the effort continues.[136]

The plurality of definitions shows that religious life is complex and varied and that it cannot be presented to people as a set ready-made meal. This need not, however, disappoint a hungry person to eat it even if some bits are bitter! In due course, people learn to prepare various dishes of their choice or invention, and there are an increasing number of cooking guides in the press and media. Finding the basic ingredients and mixing them in the right proportions are vital. Otherwise one may end up in a bad experience of eating or food poisoning. One can continue such analogies and apply them to understanding religions. While many definitions of religion stress, for example, the perception of the infinite as manifesting in uncontrollable natural forces, a unified system centred around sacred things and powers, and an inner feeling of both peace or disturbance,

---

[136] For the most famous definitions, see, I. Selvanayagam, *Religion and Religions: An Interfaith Perspective*, New Delhi: Christian World Imprints, 2018, 1-17.

they do not touch the socio-economic side of life. Karl Marx (1818-1883) put his finger on a vital nerve and pulse when he declared that 'Religious distress is at the same time the expression of real distress and the protest against real distress. Religion is the sigh of the oppressed creature, the heart of a heartless world, just as it is the spirit of a spiritless situation. It is the *opium* of the people.'[137] Volumes have been written on this definition, but it has stubbornly remained, taking different forms and challenging religion's oppressive and exploitative side. In our discussion on interreligious engagement, can we make a response together? First of all, we need to point out that just like the actual religions, Marx's vision, its practical expressions in the name of Communism and experiments, for instance, in the formation of the Soviet Union, has developed many dimensions of religion, not least the ritual and the philosophical. The utopian vision continues to remain a vision. The inherent feeling of transcendence and seeking for appropriate symbols have not been fulfilled. This is not to score points but to seek ways of working together with a proximate goal while continuing the dialogue on the ultimate goal with commitment and openness.

There is no doubt that religious visions and systems have sustained the spiritual and moral stability of millions. They will continue to do so. But at the same time religions have been the cause (or used as instruments) of conflicts and wars throughout history. In the name of God soils have been profaned and there is a possibility to sanctify them. And there are divisions in every religious tradition and some leaders thrive on them. There are even wile characters who thwart unity efforts or absorb united organisations into their sects or denominations. Moreover, religious scriptures have not been properly taught, not only the verses to be memorised, but more importantly proper approaches and interpretations. Consequently, scriptures have made some into saints, and the same scriptures have made some others into terrorists! A basic understanding of scripture is indispensable to have a healthy self-understanding and to share with friends from other religions with clarity. Also, as a great lot

[137] Quoted, Bas Wielenga, *Introduction to Marxism*, Bangalore: Centre for Social Action, 1984, 338f.

of rituals and recitations are not translated and understood in the vernacular, others are not able to appreciate them. All these will contribute to interreligious understanding and engagement.

In the interreligious pursuit of social engagement, even if a full comprehension of other religions is not possible, we should be able to find some common ground for immediate action. In 2007 a group of Muslim scholars produced a document entitled 'A Common Word between Us and You',[138] keeping Christians as their immediate partners. Since then the document has been signed by top leaders of these two religious communities, and several articles have been written and discussions organised. Basically, the document gleans from the Qur'an and Bible passages that talk about the supremacy of one God and the primacy of love. However, old chains and political incongruence continue to prevent them from moving forward to chalk out joint programmes. Of course, the word LOVE is misused and overused in interreligious parlance, and a dialogical statement of its most authentic expression has yet to emerge. Obviously, love may be sentimental, superficial, sexual, familial and in-depth sharing of the pain of others. It will be an exciting experience to share the expressions of divine love in different religious visions that can be actualised in concrete action. It is not easy to deny that in a multi-religious context love in concrete joint action alone can be the most authentic expression.

At the same time, particularly in India, truth requires all the truly religious to acknowledge that some notions are great blocks to progress in the path of development. Karma, fate, predestination and God's will are openly affirmed almost by all people. Without denouncing them there are scholars who point out that within the given there are possibilities to play our role for change. Is it possible to share such explanations and publish them in order to conscientize people? Perhaps there are still many around who know that we cannot discuss such beliefs with intellect and critical analysis. With due acknowledgement of its limit, it is important to apply the great gift of intellect and knowledge to our religious practices. Let the brain move along with the worshippers and go inside their sacred places!

---

[138] https://www.acommonword.com/the-acw-document/ as on 13 June 2018.

Otherwise superstitions will perpetuate. We often abdicate our responsibility and ask God or some transcendent power to fix things for us. We do not grow from the elementary religion of aspiring to a good life and praying for prosperity, protection and peace of mind. Interreligious engagement may come across and cause new kinds of prayer. Thereby we contribute to the credibility of religion and equip ourselves to dialogue with people of different religions and secular ideologies. In terms of vague ideas of mystery and truth which have attracted huge debates and endless claims and counter-claims, one can easily be distracted from the practical application of religious visions to concrete contexts. Similarly, we appreciate different religious experiences – crowd- ecstasy, heart-warming, mind-calming – and their positive effects. According to some religious visions, if such experiences do not lead to outgoing gestures towards others, even enemies, then their value is limited.

The World We are in

Whether religion is rejected or accepted, the present world presents many challenges for religious persons to respond. As we have already noted, in spite of many criticisms and predictions religion in one form or other or in multi-form continues to persist shaping peoples' lives and giving them some sort of meaning, though 'the meaning of meaning' may be debated. There are political pundits and ideologues. On the whole, whether humanity has become free and mature still begs a question. It is a right time to revisit the Enlightenment 'priests and prophets' who denounced religion's authority and believed that every human being will achieve unlimited and uninterrupted freedom. Some nurtured a vision of utopia on Marxian lines. Now in a new millennium what do we see and experience? It will be fruitful to ask this question and find the answer together with representatives of religious communities, secular movements and political parties. Actually, what we read in the press is not matched by religious contributions. There are areas of concern to probe. For example, it is often emphasised that freedom and responsibility should go together for a healthy person and healthy society. But what is responsible freedom? There may be fashionable ideas, but the question is about the resource to gain the will and move into experiment. True religion can certainly contribute.

In the year 2016 a new word entered into the English Dictionary, i.e., Post-Truth. It was used in reference to the lies of some world leaders and strategists which appeared to be true. It was realised more than ever before that such crooked leaders have the support of their sycophants, supporters and manipulative media. The same leader is perceived as both mad and a person of supreme mind. It is often observed that where dishonest politicians, exploitative businesses and manipulative media are in good cooperation it is detrimental for the society, particularly for the vulnerable and innocent. Not all people are able to distinguish between fact and fiction, rubies and rubbish.

The revolution of electronic communications is astonishing, and we need not repeat the chorus of their benefits. With the ideal of positivity let us not lose our intellect in critically observing what is happening. Their magnifying, mesmerising and manipulative powers seem to blind the eyes of people to see the dangers. The euphoria of the social media has subsided as it can cause ill heath and dangerous consequences. We stand speechless when we hear that mysterious networks and analytics can influence elections and other decision makings of countries thousands of miles away. Also, when we applaud achievements and heroism coming through the mass media, particularly television, those of common sense and who are conscientised may suddenly stop to give a second applause. This is due to the mindfulness that millions of youngsters around the world have no opportunity to study, train and perform their skills because they are too costly for them. The story of one or two who have come up from poor backgrounds to the limelight and the state of celebrity cannot justify keeping the majority world of young talent disabled. Moreover, the mass media might excel in style and sound, but they often lack substance in terms of truth-telling and stimulating people to assert their self-identity and self-dignity.

Commerce of commodities seems to rule the world. Normal communications are interrupted by annoying advertisements that consume time and energy, though some of its humour is entertaining. Heroic sports stars are carrying the labels on multinational co-operations, from their socks to their hats. One can be distracted by flashes, sounds and fashionable ideas. Even the first pages of respected newspapers are filled with adverts, and the disease has spread all over the world. Governments appear to be concerned about healthy food and drinks but they are not able to control the unhealthy stuffs, and the market looks unregulated. In recent years people are forced to encounter and negotiate supermarkets in every public space, and some may view them as a great facility. But one can see that the majority wade through crowded shops when they look for their boarding gates in airports. Big railway stations too have fallen into the commercial trap. No religion is averse to food and drink and decent entertainment, yet religious leaders are either silent or tolerant because they do not want to appear judgmental or moralising in the old way. Or they are enslaved to a cult which has many priests and preachers without having the guts to initiate dialogue. With extreme respect for freedom they often celebrate even suicides and, if desired, perform the priestly roles.

Wars and conflicts take away lives on a massive scale. Mass graves are discovered after a long time. We have stories of having gone out for war on the basis of misinformation. In the conflicts of wild and primitive savages the power of manual weapons was limited. Today, sophisticated weapons like aerial bombardment can kill masses over a vast area in a second. Bomb and fire power is projected as the measure of the strength of a nation. Some superpowers prosper by the production and sale of weapons to poor countries. The Secretary of such a power has said, 'Our weapons are not for storage but deployment.' Hence having the pride of thousands of military bases all over the world causing the submissive obedience of those countries or revolt by others who go for costly programmes of nuclear weapons while their masses are starving. The 'self-forgiving superpowers' still deceive people and nations by describing themselves as civilized. In a civilized world, the top leaders of two countries with massive nuclear arsenals claim that the button of one is bigger than other, to trigger and destroy. They bargain for peace while sitting on piles of nuclear bombs! Even in the 21st century we hear of spies and poisoning, etc. Are the people behind these not more brutal than the primitive savages we hear of?

Truth-speaking economists point out that a fraction of the defence budget of the nations would be enough to eradicate poverty and illiteracy in the world. If the scholarly world with the cooperation of the refined religious minds could come together to discuss a peaceful world with healthy life for all, the first task should be to write a comprehensive definition of civilization!

More than ever before, environmental concerns have come to centrestage. Earthquakes, volcanoes, storms, tsunamis, floods, drought, etc., continue to take away lives. Climate change threatens the life of the whole world. This is not the place to give an analysis of human greed extending far beyond need in consumption. We know how wars and bombings destroy the integration and health of the environment. To go into the issue deeper we need to have the perception of the complex bundle of knots that human aggression has created over the centuries and millennia. To say that God or the divine power is in control is not enough because obviously humans have the enormous responsibility to mend the creation and maintain its balance. Scrapyards and wastage fills of the so called developed world pose a threat. In some cases, unwanted or dated tools are transported to the developing world at great cost with a sense of charity. When clothes spill out from wardrobes they may reach jumble sales and charity shops. Chunks of ever increasing sheets of newspapers (with considerable space taken for adverts), used books and other papers some of which litter the public spaces and paths are recycled, but without asking if we need them all and looking for alternative ways of controlling their number and the pest of commercial adverts. The toxin of plastic and its poisonous effect on water and atmosphere is recognised as needing action. Self-control is a common term, but religions have explained its enormity and methods. It is over-all control of life, not just muscle-relaxation and mind control. It is the outcome of some sort of enlightened awareness or mindfulness and contentment. It is argued that this mental and emotional condition would help to tackle the menace of increasing gun crimes, knife crimes, teenage pregnancy and mental illness.

The India we are in

On the whole India, with the largest democracy and second largest population in the world of over 1.2 billion, continues to baffle most visitors and many of its citizens. It is said to be mystery, magic, miracle and magnet. An observation of a perceptive outsider with long first-hand experience: 'Take India. There may be breath-taking inequalities and injustices but it is hard not be optimistic in a country that bubbles with activity and enthusiasm.'[139] With different religions, cultures and languages it has adopted a secular polity. But 'being religious' and 'being secular' in India has an unbelievable meaning and practice. For example, the United Kingdom is nominally religious (Christian with a monarch as the head) but phenomenally secular, whereas its former colony India is nominally secular and phenomenally religious! Economically, it is classed among the 'developing countries,' but one can easily see that the first world, second world and third world are rolling round together posing both beauty and brokenness. For achieving greater economic justice and life committed to secular principles, religious communities and secular thinkers need to work together though its path and goals are not clear.

In India there is a secular Constitution but not necessarily a secular Consciousness. Secularism (from the Latin word *saeculum*=the ordinary, the related word *saecularis*=the world or being worldly, or *saecularis*=materialism) is basically a moral philosophy covering all people and their ordinary or worldly life without the control of religion. India inherited western secularism through British colonialism with little adjustment. Religio-political thinkers repeatedly point out that Indian secularism is not like western secularism (irreligious, anti-religious, etc.) but that it is not based on or favouring one religion. But over the years, particularly since Independence in 1947, communal conflicts with beastly violence, using religion for gaining block votes in political elections, domination of the people of major religion and the moaning and manipulating tactics of minorities, etc., have raised questions about the nature and manifestation of secularism in India.

139 Justin Rowlatt, "Leaving India and the best shave in the world" https://www.bbc.co.uk/news/world-asia-india-44449607, as on 16/6/18.

There are continuing debates[140] and the positions include outright rejection as irrelevant, indigenization and education, political will and determination for creative and fair treatment of all, recognition of traditional values which have been intertwined and even confused with modern, and implementation of the Constitution with principled distance and so on. In essence, what is needed is a common vision, equality, fairness and political will.

Can religions come together upholding secularism? At times of crisis every religious group comes up with its particular understanding of secularism and in most cases theirs is not averse to secular principles. Common humanity is affirmed with the repeated indication of commonality in facing hunger, ill-health and death. But the problem becomes acute when the judiciary is suspected of religious favouritism, misuse of the Freedom of Religion as fundamental right (without realising the conditional clause: subject to health, morality and public order) and acts of violence in the name of restoring properties and worship places even if there is no strong evidence about original ownership. There are some particular issues which are protracted, mainly in the case of concessional reservation from which certain religious minorities are excluded,[141] a uniform civil code (replacing existing Personal

---

[140] See, Densingh Oliver, "Understanding Religion and Spirituality in Current Debates on Secularism in India", in *Religion, Spirituality & Secularity in Multi-Religious India*, ed. by I. Selvanayagam, New Delhi: Christian World Imprints, 2017, 97-108.

[141] According to a Presidential Order of 1950 those Dalit converts from Hinduism were excluded from the privileges of the Scheduled Caste (name used by the British and continued to be used even after Independence). Particularly the Muslim and Christian Dalits argued that their religion was not able to change their economic condition and therefore should be treated as eligible for the privilege of positive discrimination. Later it was restored to Sikhs in 1956 and for Buddhists in 1990, as they were regarded as closely associated with or even sub-sects of Hinduism. Muslim and Christian Dalits have been engaged in a prolonged struggle, involving even figures like Mother Theresa. Few leaders including the former Prime Minister V.P. Singh promised to remove this unjust impediment for Muslim and Christian Dalits but his ministry was toppled and later he died of illness. One fear was that the continuation of privileges even after conversion encourage Hindu Dalits to convert while the 'Ghar wapsi'(= back to home) programme has been launched by the revivalist Hindu movements to convert people from other religions to Hinduism.

Law), and the settlement of the Kashmir issue. Unfortunately, religious communities are party to the problem, unwilling to become the solution.

Religious behaviour in public spheres has raised questions. Can political leaders worship in their worship places with the government paraphernalia? Should religious symbols and portraits be installed in government offices? At functions such as ground-breaking ceremonies for a public building, dedication and opening the shutters of dams, etc., can religious rituals be performed? Is the prophetic exhortation of Jawaharlal Nehru, the first Prime Minister of India, a fanatic of secularist, about confining religion to the individual sphere and treating public facilities such as dams our new sacred places, forgotten? Gandhi, who remained stubbornly religious (Hindu) differed from Nehru and argued that religion should be in the public sphere as a mirror of moral consciousness. Those who claim to have the secular consciousness with or without religious commitment can prove to be authentic only when they come together to share for clarity and educating the public.

Educated Indians and half-baked intellectuals often come up with an exaggerated acclamation of India's antiquity as if sanctity lies in it. Because of their influence, students and even ordinary people are brain-washed to affirm how wonderful was India's past. The so-called communal historiography has caused much tension in the recent past. But no question is asked about the present problem of nation-building and secularism-maintaining. There is a place for reading and writing history, but it is dangerous to become slaves of history. This generation can have the proud credit of changing history for a better future of India. Also, it is uncreative to be struck with iconic figures of the past including heroes and saints, and to take their words as scripture. Every religious community must look at their iconic figures critically with a view to moving forward. For example, Gandhi who defined religion in terms of Truth and Non-violence engaged in an honest experiment with truth. But truth requires us to admit that he struggled to bring together different threads to coherence. His view and commitment to non-violence had anomalies, loopholes and even elements of ignorance.[142] A new fundamental openness is called for for collective experiment with truth by crystallising and mobilising all the good visions and thoughts behind religion and secularism in India. Without simply leaving for politicians and communalists, those who have secular consciousness and confidence in every religious community need to form networks for discussion and dissemination. Such engagement would bring respect to their religion, beyond beliefs, practices and property management.

From Charity to Struggle in Solidarity

Charity means voluntary giving to those in need, often through organs and organisations with that purpose, act of benevolence, tolerance and courtesy. Almost all the religions have charity work and organisations. 'There are more than 185,000 registered charities in England and Wales. The number is rising by 5,000 a year…The Charity Commission lists 620 cancer charities alone and more than 200 charities working with homeless people just in London…No wonder 70% of the public think there are too many charities doing similar work and competing with each other, according to new ICM opinion poll figures. The poll was carried out for the Media Trust, which is today staging a debate on charity proliferation and duplication, asking whether confidence in the sector is being crucially undermined.'[143] The population of England and Wales is about 60 million. 'A total number of registered projects across India has reached around 25,000. Officials have shared that out of all registered ongoing projects across the country, as many as 16,125 projects have been registered in Maharashtra. Maha RERA has registered over

---

[142] For an analysis, see, I. Selvanayagam, "Gandhi's Interpretation of Ahimsa: A Re-View" in *Enhancing Our Home: Re-Reading and Re-Living Gandhian Thought*, ed. by Johnson J. Puthenpurackal, Bangalore: Asian Trading Corporation, 2016, 56-75.

[143] The poll was carried out for the Media Trust, with the support of *The Guardian* https://www.theguardian.com/society/2000/nov/08/guardiansocietysupplement5 as on 15/6/18.

14,000 agents under the Act. 30 Apr 2018.[144] Besides, over a million operate under Companies Act and some of them include charity works.[145] There may be several unregistered charities of small scale. The kinds and level of contributions are varied. Obviously, legacies are a major source of income as are in some cases donations of wealthy persons. In India, the names of certain philanthropists are attached to some projects. The hardworking collectors of contributions in both contexts are appreciable. Only a separate study can reveal the fact of the sources of income for the charities.

However, the above-mentioned observation in the case of England and Wales is significant, i.e., 'charity proliferation and duplication, asking whether confidence in the sector is being crucially undermined'. In such and other contexts slogans such as 'Prevention is better than cure', 'Public health is more important than ambulance service', 'When one asks for fish, teach fishing' and 'Peacemaking is more vital than rescue and rehabilitation work'. This is not to undermine the involvement in crisis, created by natural calamities. Also, it should be recognised that the meaning of charity is understood in more comprehensive and inclusive senses, for example, from loving the stranger and supporting the struggle against tyrannies. What is warned of is complacency, self-righteousness and failure to question and tackle the root causes that perpetuate poverty, inequality and injustice. It is not enough to kill the brood while feeding the serpent!

The parable of the Good Samaritan is widely known irrespective of religious adherences. Many years ago, I suggested an Indian extension to this parable. In this version, when the Samaritan

---

[144] Maha RERA accounts 65 percent of total registered projects – 99 Acres https://www.99acres.com/.../maharera-accounts-65-percent-of-total-registered-projects-n...https://www.google.co.uk/search?ei=ftkgW5CwEJHJwQKm3JWQAg &q=Number+of+Registered+Projects+in+India&oq=Number+of+Registered+Projects+in+India&gs_l=psy-ab.3...38774.44765.0.46964.18.18.0.0.0.0.202.1847.11 j6j1.18.0..2..0...1.1.64.psy-ab..0.11.1266...35i39k1j33i10k1.0.wUPt3kxxb1U as on 15/6/18.

[145] https://economictimes.indiatimes.com/news/economy/policy/number-of-registered-companies-climbs-to-15-27-lakh-in-january/articleshow/51026331.cms as on 13/6/18.

was passing that way next time he saw two victims of wayside robbery lying on the ground and took them to the inn. The number increased in the course of his further visits and the capacity of the inn was overstretched. The Samaritan decided that the only way to stop these robberies was to report them to the police, which he did. But to his horror, the next time he saw more victims and detected collaboration between the police and the robbers. Then he took the matter to the court, and the struggle in solidarity with the victims was on. I concluded that by helping incidentally those in need we prove to be Good Samaritans; by asking the cause of the same need increasing we become better Samaritans; and by identifying with the victims and continuing the struggle we change to become the best Samaritans.

When in the UK institutional racism was publicly admitted, irresponsible sex creating problems for the society and the increase in crime are left to the authorities and the police to deal with. The religious communities are on the whole silent about the moral side of it, and one wishes that they would take these issues as part of their commitments and that interreligious engagement were promoted to analyse the cause of such problems. In India, while there is no dearth of slogans on justice, equality and peaceful existence, in spite of reform movements, caste and untouchability continues to thrive. There has been international lobbying to cover up the serpent. In England there was a study which revealed caste discrimination and practice of untouchability among the Indian Diaspora in the country. It is heartening that the Dalit Solidarity Network in UK and similar secular movements around the world create awareness and initiate action. Many thought that globalization would help abolish caste, but rather as it has turned out caste is globalized! Apart from daily discrimination and harassment, the untouchable Dalits are subjected to untold suffering. The current issue is lynching for beef eating, and this has terrorised vulnerable people across the religions. Whether cow protection is religious, cultural or casteist, the collective good will of the Indian people can be tested only by their coming together with commitment and openness. Often political preaching repeats the ideal of non-violence in order to stifle the legitimate agitation of the poor and victims of injustice. The mantra 'unity in diversity' is recited loudly, but there is no clarification about divisions and demons in the diversity. Can poverty and caste-age-gender discrimination, etc., be part of diversity?

While the image of a fair-skinned, silk sari-ed and beautiful 'Mother India' is projected, informed people are painfully aware that over 25% of Indians live below the poverty line[146] and that more than 75% defecate in public. Most public toilets are stinking without proper maintenance. 'Clean India Mission' was inaugurated in October 2014 as a campaign to clean rivers such as the Ganges, roads and streets and to construct toilets in rural areas. The budget was great, but the effect has yet to be measured. More than cleaning the water, soil and roadways, it has been pointed out that the corruption that has poisoned the bureaucracy needs to be cleaned with radical methods. Despite the celebrated Right to Information, ordinary people have to travel long distances and even have to stay overnight to get a letter or signature. Religious institutions are not exempted. In many cases public sight of bribery in work uniform could not be challenged though exposed repeatedly in the mass media. It is a fact that individual challengers have to pay unbearable costs, but groups and masses can work for change. The greatest processions in India are religious, and if they can be mobilised to challenge corruption and untouchability, religion will have its due respect. Diplomatic parlours and protocol speeches of leaders with unbearable repetition seem to have no meaning. We have not yet cleared off outlawed practices such as child marriage, widow burning, manual scavenging and temple prostitution.

Just like giving to charities in the UK, giving to the poor (particularly to beggars) in India takes the form of alms often done with reverence, and the main aim is merit-earning for the giver's benefit here and hereafter. Struggle in solidarity transcends simple charity and almsgiving. Few religious visions are worth pursuing in this connection. Swami Vivekananda (1863-1902), a Hindu reformer and liberation theologian, after his foot journey across India in which he encountered the masses in skeleton frames, declared

---

[146] The poverty line has been varied and an accurate figure is not given. However, the current rate is around 1,000 rupees per month (=approximately £12).

God to be in the form of the poor. The Ramakrishna Mission was partly based on this vision. There is another vision that essentially God is in solidarity with the victims of injustice and the vulnerable. Such visions certainly contradict visions of an unmoved mover and lover of ritual sacrifice but interreligious dialogue with commitment to uplift the weakest at the bottom and with openness to consider new visions of God has yet to take place. Such a vision comes close to many secular visions. For instance, C.N. Annadurai (1909-1969), the founder of the DMK ('Dravidian Progressive Movement') and a former chief minister of Tamil Nadu famously said, 'See God in the smile of the poor.' His ministry initiated (in 1967) a new era and a 'concrete reconstruction', and its secularism had a taint of agnosticism and atheism. His political heir M. Karunanidhi (1924-2018), a twelve term member of the legislative assembly and five-time chief minister of Tamil Nadu, who contributed enormously to a cultural renaissance and societal reconstruction of the state, tried to challenge the agelong caste discrimination and the sources that perpetuated poverty through his writings (including 75 film stories with dialogues) and speeches. But taking advantage of Anna's untimely death in 1969 and taking on Karunanidhi's challenges, dominant religious forces (taking advantage of mainly illiterate masses, one side of cinema and distorted views of history) crept in, neutralising their movement and breaking it into pieces, though it has survived. In any case, this is another story, one of the many such stories in India.

The above reflections may look simple ramblings. However, the intention is to stimulate more systematic writing with clearer vision and solid proposals for concrete action. As a conclusion, let me point out that religious communities and leaders in India (perhaps elsewhere too) have failed to engage in conversation with those with secular visions or ideologies and with social activists. An empirical study will establish if they lack confidence, fear further exposure of their religion's weakness or superstition, or are already crippled by embarrassment at the fierce criticism in the public discourse and media. It is ironical that social/cultural movements such as DMK (now a political party) are basically atheistic or agnostic although most of masses of their adherents are religious in one way or other, and this is exploited by religious leaders. At the same time, some atheist leaders' extraordinary and exemplary life and service have earned them a name that matches the best elements of religion. For example, Udhayakiri Swamy, a respected Hindu sage, paid homage at the tomb of Karananidhi who died on 7 August 2018, and he then openly observed that though an atheist he stressed love, embrace of inclusivity and modesty and did much good for people and 'in fact he too is a sage' (*citthar*).[147] What can we say about such cases? If there is any conviction that the present society (and the world) can be made better and people's lives fuller, interreligious cooperation and cooperation between religious communities and secular movements is indispensable. If the religious persons withdraw into shells in the name of spirituality but come out to preach morality without any appeal to socio-economic realities, certainly they are the losers. On the contrary, interreligious engagement for socio-economic reconstruction may result in enormous benefit and create opportunities for relationship and dialogue with secular movements. There should be no pre-conditions apart from the shared affirmation of the *mul-mantra*, 'commitment and openness.'

---

[147]https://www.dailythanthi.com/News/State/2018/08/11022604/Karunanidhi-Samadhi-Actors-Karthi-Vijayakumar-Anjali.vpf; *'citthar' represents a group of wandering bards in the Tamil tradition who transcended religion and propagated rational thinking and liberative ideas.*

Author's English Publications on Interreligious Relations

Books

1. *Towards a Humanist Theology of Religious Harmony - Insights from the Writings of Dayanandan Francis*, Madras: CLS, 1994.
2. *Dialogue on Dialogue - Reflections on Inter-faith Encounters*, Madras: CLS, 1995.
3. Ed. (Authored 20 articles), *Biblical Insights on Inter-faith Dialogue*, Bangalore: BTTBPSA-BTESSC, 1995.
4. *Gospel and Culture in Tamilnadu*, Geneva: WCC, 1996.
5. *The Dynamics of Hindu Religious Traditions - Teape Lectures on Sacrifice, Gita and Dialogue*, Bangalore: Asian Trading Corporation, 1996.
6. *A Second Call – Ministry and Mission in a Multifaith Milieu*, Madras (Chennai): The Christian Literature Society, 2000.
7. *Relating to People of Other Faiths: Insights from the Bible*, Thiruvalla: Christava Sahitya Samithi, BTTBPSA, 2004.
8. Ed. with a chapter "The Parable of the Prodigal Son: A Contextual Reading" (203-209), *Light on Our Dusty Path: Essays for a Bible Lover*, Bangalore: BTESSC/SATHRI, 2008.

9. (with S. Amirtham) *Glimpses into Life:* New Delhi: ISPCK, No.9. *Inter-faith Encounters* (2015); *10. Truth and Reconciliation* (2016).
10. *Being Evangelical and Dialogical: A Healthy Balance in a Multifaith Context*, Delhi: ISPCK, 2012.
11. *Kristu Bhakti and Krishna Bhakti: A Christian-Hindu Dialogue Contributing to Comparative Theology*, New Delhi: Christian World Imprints, 2017.
12. Ed. *Religion, Spirituality & Secularity in Multi-Religious India: Visions and Experiments*, New Delhi: Christian World Imprints, 2017; with "Preface" (xi – xv), Chapter 2. "Defining Religion in Hindu India" (13 – 26); Chapter 11. "Human Sex, Sacred or Profane?: Hindu – Christian Perceptions" (127 – 140).
13. *Religion and Religions: An Interfaith Perspective*, New Delhi: Christian World Imprints, 2018.

Articles

14. "The Centrality of Cross in Dialogue", *International Review of Mission*, LXXIV/296, Oct., 1985.
15. "Towards a Dialogical Approach to Reality and Religions", *Arasaradi Journal of Theological Reflection*, I/2, 1985, 24-33.
16. "Is Religious Conversion Possible in the Process of Inter-Faith Dialogue?", *Discernment*, III/2 Autumn, 1989, 2-11.
17. "The Tension between Mission and Dialogue: Some Observations",*MASIHI SEVAK*, Vol. XIV, 1989, 1-6.
18. (With S. Gangadharan) "Learning with People of Other Faiths", *Venturing into Life, 20 Years of TTS Story*, ed. by S. Amirtham & C.R.W. David, Madurai: TTS Publications, 1990, 97-108.
19. "Hindu-Christian Dialogue in India: Some Recent Developments", *The Challenge of Dialogue, Papers from the Meeting of the Dialogue Workshop*, Casablanca/Morocco, June 1989, WCC, 72-77.
20. "Communalism in Contemporary India: A Christian Response from Dialogical Perspective", *Arasaradi Journal of Theological Reflection*, Vol. III, No.2, July-Dec., 1990, 21-25.

21. "Floating Ark and Shipwreck: Contrary Biblical Models for Multi-Faith Context and Christian Living", *Asia Journal of Theology*, 5/2, Oct., 1991, 338-345.
22. (With Dr. S. Gangadharan), "The Communion of Saints: Christian and Tamil Saiva Perspectives", *Hindu Christian Studies Bulletin*, Vol.5, 1992, 13-19; *Voices from the Margin*, ed. R. S. Sugirtharajah, Orbis/SPCK, 1995, pp. 381-393.
23. "Inter-Faith Dialogue: A Clarification of Perspectives and Issues", *Current Dialogue*, WCC, No.23, Dec., 1992, 20-25; *THE SATHRI JOOURNAL*, 1/1993, 22-29.
24. Edited and contributed an essay on "Non-Biblical Literary Resources for Theological Writing in India", *The Multi-Faith Context of India - Resources and Challenges for Christians*, Bangalore: BTTBPSA, 1992, 24-40.
25. "Inter-religious Communication - The Primary Blockades on the Way", *Arasaradi Journal of Theological Reflection*, V/162, 1992, 183-194.
26. "Who is this Jesus? - A Biblical Outline for Clearer Self-Understanding and Communication in a Multi-faith Context", *Asia Journal of Theology*, 7/2 Oct., 1993, 231-243.
27. "Jewish-Christian Relationship from a Third World Perspective", *Current Dialogue*, No. 25, Dec., 1993, 20-31.
28. The Ayodhya Issue: A Review from a Dialogical Perspective", *National Council of Churches Review*, Vol.CXIV, No.2, Feb., 1994, 123-134.
29. *Evangelism and Inter Faith Dialogue - Are they Incompatible or Complementary?*, Occasional Paper No.13, Selly Oak Colleges, Birmingham,1993. Indian Edition: Thiruvalla: CSS, 1996.
30. "Challenges to Religious Pluralism in India: The Nature of Hindu Fundamentalism", *Challenges to Religious Pluralism*, ed. A. Pushparajan, Madurai Arch Diocese: The Commission for Dialogue, 1994, 28-38.
31. "People of God and Peoples of God: Asian Christian Discussions" and "An Indian Christian View of Religious Pluralism" in *People of God, Peoples of God, A Jewish -Christian Conversation in Asia*, ed. Hans Ucko, Geneva: WCC, 1996, 67-83, 100-110.

32. *"People of God, Peoples of God" A WCC Consultation on The Church and Jewish People*, Budapest - Oct., 15-21, 1994, ed. by Rabbi Leon Klenicki, Anti-Deformation League & CCJP, 37-48.
33. "Pastoral Counselling for Creative Encounters with the People of Other Faiths", *Arasaradi Journal of Theological Reflection*, VIII/1 & 2 (Jan.-Dec.), 1995, 40-60.
34. "Inter-religious dialogue and national integration: A Christian Viewpoint", *THE BULLETIN* (Henry Martin Institute of Islamic Studies), 16/3&4, July-Dec., 1996, 106-111.
35. "Christian Theology and Mission in the Midst of Many Theologies and Missions", Lutheran World Federation *DOCUMENTATION* 41/1997 - Theological Perspectives on Other Faiths, Geneva: LWF, 1997, 181-201.
36. "Mission in a Pluralist Society", in *Greater Peace, Closer Fellowship, and Fuller Life*, ed. by Lily & Sam Amirtham, CSI Golden Jubilee Publications, Madras, 1997, 216-225.
37. "Anglicans and Inter-faith Relations - A historical retrospect" in *Anglicanism - A Global Communion*, ed. by Andrew Wingate, et. al. London: Mowbray, 1998, 341-346.
38. "Commitment and Openness in a Multifaith Context", *Thinking Mission*, USPG 'Sharing Faith in Today's World', December, 1999.
39. "Towards an Evangelical Theology for a Pluralist Age" in *Mission at the Dawn of the 21st Century – A Vision for the Church*, ed. Paul Varo Martinson, Minneapolis: Kirk House Publishers, 1999, 201-218.
40. "Death by Dialogue: The End of Denominational Theology – A World Church Perspective", *Epworth Review*, 27/1, Jan., 2000, 84-93.
41. "Identity, Inspiration, Interpretation and Insights: The Significance of the Christian Scripture in the Midst of Scriptures", in *Bible Speaks Today* (Essays in honour of Gnana Robinson, ed. by Daniel Jones Muthunayagam, Delhi: ISPCK (for UTC Bangalor)e, 2000, 224-241.
42. "Crossing Over and Coming Back: Evangelical Openness and Dialogical Witness in a Multi-faith Context", in *A Great*

Commission – Christian Hope in Religious Diversity, ed. by Martin Forward, Stephen Plant and Susan White, Bern: Peter Lang, 2000, 267-279.

43. "TRUTH and truths in Inter-faith Dialogue", *Religion and Society*, 46/1-2, March-June, 1999, 37-64.
44. "A Study of the Life of Abraham" in *Approaches, Foundations, Issues and Models of Interfaith Relations*, ed. by David Emmanuel Sing and Robert Edwin Schick, Delhi: ISPCK&HMI, 2001, 372-378.
45. "The Bible and Non-Christian Scriptures", *Epworth Review*, 29/1 Jan., 2002, 49-58.
46. "Re-reading John 14:6 in the Context of Two Recent Events in the UK" *Current Dialogue*, No. 40, Dec., 2002, 44-51.
47. "Theological Positions in Christian Approach to Religious Pluralism – The Fourth Way", *Arasaradi Journal of Theological Reflection*, XVII/1, Jan-June, 2004, 1-23.
48. "Interfaith Dialogue" (chapter 7) in *A History of the Ecumenical Movement*, Vol. 3 (1968 – 2000), ed. by John Briggs, Mercy Amba Oduyoye and Georges Tsetsis, Geneva: WCC, 2004, 149-174.
49. "Editorial: The Quest for Spirituality in the Secular Multi-faith Context of India", *Implicit Religion*, 8/2, July, 2005, pp. 101-117.
50. "Encountering the Hindus: The Legacy of Ziegenbalg" in *Halle and the Beginning of Christianity in India*, Vol. II: *Christian Mission in the Context*, ed. by A. Gross, Y.V. Kumaradoss and H. Liebau, Halle: Franckeschen, 2006, 903-922.
51. "Truth and Reconciliation: An Interfaith Perspective", *International Journal of Public Theology*, Volume 1 Issue 3/4, 2007.
52. Gandhi on Non-Violence – Does Merton's Appreciation have any Appeal today? *The Merton Journal*, EASTERTIDE, 14/1, 2007, 2-14.
53. "Interfaith Dialogue in India and England: A Personal Reflection", *Pilgrim*, No. 31, August, 2007, 7-13.
54. "Getting into Real: Religious Commitment and Interfaith Dialogue", *Interreligious Insight*, 6/1, Jan., 2008, 37-42.

55. "The Hindu Diaspora in the UK: Insights and Challenges for Christian Mission", in *Mission and Migration*, Hope Valley: Cliff College, 2008, 95-108
56. "Truth and Reconciliation – An Interfaith Perspective from India" in *Peace and Reconciliation: In Search of Shared Identity*, ed. by Sebastian Kim, Pauline Kollontai and Greg Hoyland, Farnham: Ashgate, 2008, 35-49.
57 "Revisiting the Unknown Christ of Hinduism: A Tribute to Raymundo Panikkar", *Gurukul Journal of Theological Studies*, XXI/2, June, 2010, 61-70.
58. "Christian Mission in the Midst of Many Missions" in *Participating in God's Mission Today*, ed. by Santhosh Kumar, Thiruvalla: Christava Sahitya Samithi& UTC Bangalore, 2011, 38-56.
59. "Guidelines for Christians on Interfaith Dialogue in India: Some Notes" in *Theology Beyond Neutrality: Essays to Honour Wesley Ariarajah*, ed. by Marshal Fernando and Robert Crusz, Colombo: Ecumenical Institute, 2011, 103-116; *NCC Review*, CXXX1/11, Dec., 2011, 38-56.
60. "Paradigms of Religious Pluralism: A Clarification", *Ariopagus: Journal of the Association of Faculty for Religion, Philosophy and Culture*, Vol. 1, 2011, 75-84.
61. "Majestic Elephant and Menacing Mouse: An Observation of Hindu-Christian Relationships in India" in *Among the People: Essays in Honour of Rev. Dr. P. G. Vargis*, ed. by V.D. John &Viju Wilson, Delhi: ISPCK & Hoshangabad: SALT, 2012, 95-100.
62. "Disability: An Interfaith Perspective" in *Sprouts of Disability Theology*, ed. by Christopher Rajkumar, Nagpur: NCCI, 2012, 21-30.
63. "Jewish-Christian Theological Rapprochement: Insights from the Book of Revelation", *Gurukul Journal of Theological Studies*, XXIII/1 Jan., 2012, 50-64.
64. "Commitment and Openness in a Multifaith Context", *Religion and Society*, 57/4, Dec., 2012, 62-73.
65. "Swami Vivekananda: A Hindu Liberation Theologian" in *The Yobel Spring, vol. 2* (Festschrift to Rev. Dr. Chilkuri Vasantha Rao on his 50th birthday), ed. by Praveen PS Perumalla,

Royce M. Victor and Naveen Rao, ISPCK (Delhi) and ACTC (Hyderabad), 2014, 723-734.

66. "Interrogating the Idea of Hybridity from an Interfaith Perspective", *Current Dialogue*, No. 57, December, 2015, 41-49.
67. "Journeying Together with People of Other Faiths in God's Mission", *Religion and Society*, 61/1&2, March-June, 2016, 88-102.
68. "Gandhi's Interpretation of Ahimsa: A Re-View" in *Enhancing Our Home: Re-Reading and Re-Living Gandhian Thought*, ed. by Johnson J. Puthenpurackal, Bengaluru: Asian Trading Corporation (with Association of Christian Philosophers in India), 2016, 56-75.

Book Reviews and Short Articles

1. "Inter-Faith Dialogue: Some Programme Models", *Indian Missiological Review*, Vol. 13, No.2, July 1991, 48-54.
2. A. Pushparajan, *From Conversion to Fellowship*, in *Gandhi-marq*, 15/1, April-June 1993, 96-98.
3. "Role of Religions in Secular India", *UNITE*, Madurai, 1/2, Dec. 1993, 96-98.
4. Hans Kung's *Tracing the Way-Spiritual Dimensions of the world Religions* in *Epworth Review*, Jan 2003, 90-91.
5. J.W. Bowker (ed.), *Conflict and Reconciliation: The Contribution of Religions*, in *Gurukul Journal of Theological Studies*, XXII/1, January 2011, 16-122.
6. "Interfaith Dialogue: Perennial Questions, Yet Journeying with Provisional Answers", Editorial, *Gurukul Journal of Theological Studies*, XXII/1, January 2011, 2-8
7. A. Bongiovanni, L. Fernando and Edwin, eds., *Dialogue in a Pluralist World*, Delhi: ISPCK, 2013, xi + 190, *Asia Journal of Theology*, 28/2, October 2014, 304-307.
8. "Yoga-Yaga-Tyaga", *People's Reporter*, 28/21 Nov. 10-25, 2015, 3, 5.
9. "Reflections on Hindu-Christian Relations: A Response to Anantanand Rambachan" in *Relating with Hindu Diaspora:*

Anglican & Lutheran Reflections, ed. by Lucinda Mosher, Andrew Wingate & Joshva Raja, London, UK: A joint publication of Anglican Interfaith Networks, Lutheran Purvoo Communion & World Council of Churches, 2015, 7-10.

Index of Personal Names